MAKING SOFTWARE
DEVELOPMENT VISIBLE

WILEY SERIES IN
SOFTWARE ENGINEERING PRACTICE

Series Editors:

Patrick A.V. Hall, *Brunel University, UK*
Martyn A. Ould, *Praxis Systems plc, UK*
William E. Riddle, *Software Design & Analysis, Inc., USA*

Fletcher J. Buckley • Implementing Software Engineering Practices
John J. Marciniak and Donald J. Reifer • Software Acquisition
Management
John S. Hares • SSADM for the Advanced Practitioner
Martyn A. Ould • Strategies for Software Engineering
The Management of Risk and Quality
David P. Youll • Making Software Development Visible
Effective Project Control
Charles P. Hollocker • Software Reviews and Audits Handbook

MAKING SOFTWARE DEVELOPMENT VISIBLE

Effective Project Control

David P. Youll

JOHN WILEY & SONS
Chichester • New York • Brisbane • Toronto • Singapore

Other Wiley Editorial Offices

John Wiley & Sons, Inc., 605 Third Avenue,
New York, NY 10158-0012, USA

Jacaranda Wiley Ltd, G.P.O. Box 859, Brisbane,
Queensland 4001, Australia

John Wiley & Sons (Canada) Ltd, 22 Worcester Road,
Rexdale, Ontario M9W 1L1, Canada

John Wiley & Sons (SEA) Pte Ltd, 37 Jalan Pemimpin 05-04,
Block B, Union Industrial Building, Singapore 2057

Library of Congress Cataloging-in-Publication Data:
Youll, David P.
     Making software development visible : effective project control /
David P. Youll.
         p.   cm. — (Wiley series in software engineering practice)
     Includes bibliographical references and index.
     ISBN 0 471 92746 5
     1. Computer software—Development.   I. Title.   II. Series.
QA76.76.D47Y67   1990
005.1'068'4—dc20   90-42922
                                                                          CIP

British Library Cataloguing in Publication Data:
Youll, David P.
     Making software development visible : effective project
     control. – (Wiley series in software engineering practice)
     I. Title
     005.1

     ISBN 0 471 92746 5

Printed in Great Britain by Courier International Ltd, Tiptree, Essex.

To my wife, Kate

CONTENTS

PREFACE   xv

1   INTRODUCTION   1

What is the role of a manager?   2
Why is there a need for visibility?   3
Critical questions for managers   4
What should a project manager have visibility of?   6
How visibility is obtained   10
Structure of this book   13

2   FORWARD VISIBILITY   17

Introduction   17
The elements of a plan   20
Estimating   22
Contingency and minimising risk   24
Targets   25
Work Breakdown Structures   26
Analysis of plans   26
Organisation Visibility   35
Planning to achieve quality targets   36
Strategy for planning   37
Benefits and visibility provided by plans   41

3   VISIBILITY OF PROGRESS   43

Introduction   43
Progress visibility by monitoring the utilisation of resources   45
    Slip charts   45
    Balls on the walls   46
    Accuracy of estimating   48
    Resource utilisation in a period   49
    Resource utilisation - cumulative   51
    Evolution of budgeted costs and end date   55
    Utilisation of hardware resources   57
Progress visibility by monitoring the creation of components   58
    Production in a period   58
    Cumulative counts of production   60
Procedures   64
Benefits provided by progress monitoring   64

4   PRODUCT QUALITY   65

Introduction   66
Monitoring reviews and tests   67
    Reviews and tests in a period   68
    Number of reviews before success   69
    Defects found in products   70
    Thoroughness of verification and validation   72
Problems and changes   77
    Problems and changes in a period   81
    Cumulative problems and changes   85
    Effectiveness of clearing problems and changes   89
Software quality metrics   90
System and application quality   93
    Reusability   94
    Software structure   95
    System metrics   97
    Reliability and availability   97
When should a product be released?   99

5 SUPPORT VISIBILITY   101

Computing facilities   101
Organisation facilities   103
Sub-contracts   107

6 PROCESS VISIBILITY   109

Comparing the results of projects   110
Understanding the process   112
   Rework   113
   The cost of change 114
   What was the cause of a change? 116
Monitoring the resource utilisation   120

7 VISIBILITY OF MAINTENANCE   123

Time to respond to a problem report   123
Time to correct problems   125
The customer's view of product quality 127
Categories of problems   127
Cost of Maintenance   129

8 IMPLEMENTING VISIBILITY   133

Managing visibility   133
Selecting metrics   134
Preparing the procedures   136
   Automation   137
   Organisation   138
Preparing people   141
Introducing visibility   142
Replanning   145
End of project reviews   145
Costs   146
Benefits   147

What next?   148
Conclusions   150

Appendix CHOOSING AND USING
GRAPHS   **151**

Comparison of components to the whole   152
Comparison of items   154
Comparison of items over time   156
Co-relationship between variations   156
Summary   157

INDEX   **159**

LIST OF FIGURES

Figure 1.1:   The manager in a closed loop control situation
Figure 1.2:   Visibility over the project
Figure 1.3:   Graph showing actual costs and planned costs v. time
Figure 1.4:   Graph showing predicted end date

Figure 2.1:   Estimate compared to budget and deadline
Figure 2.2:   Work Breakdown Structure
Figure 2.3:   A PERT network
Figure 2.4:   Network showing critical path
Figure 2.5:   Resources required for a project
Figure 2.6:   Typical profile of resources used on a project
Figure 2.7:   A Gantt chart
Figure 2.8:   A personnel plan
Figure 2.9:   An organisation chart
Figure 2.10:   Information flow in an organisation
Figure 2.11:   Production plan
Figure 2.12:   Planned rate of production
Figure 2.13:   Cost - schedule tradeoffs

Figure 3.1:   Slip chart
Figure 3.2:   Balls on the walls
Figure 3.3:   Correlation of actual costs with planned
Figure 3.4:   Weekly costs and achievement

Figure 3.5:   Planned and actual progress
Figure 3.6:   Planned, actual and earned progress
Figure 3.7:   Cumulative costs
Figure 3.8:   Historical view of predicted final costs
Figure 3.9:   Historical view of predicted end date
Figure 3.10:   Compilation rate
Figure 3.11:   Weekly production of products
Figure 3.12:   Programming plans/progress
Figure 3.13:   Test data plans/progress
Figure 3.14:   Progress of testing

Figure 4.1:   Set of paths through a software product
Figure 4.2:   Reviews in each period
Figure 4.3:   Number of reviews before success
Figure 4.4:   Defects found in modules
Figure 4.5:   Defect frequencies
Figure 4.6:   Test coverage of a system
Figure 4.7:   Test coverage achieved by modules
Figure 4.8:   Coverage of tests
Figure 4.9:   Failures per hour
Figure 4.10:   Problem report form
Figure 4.11:   Change authorisation form
Figure 4.12:   Outstanding problems and changes in each period
Figure 4.13:   Rework outstanding and completed in each period
Figure 4.14:   Progress of problems in each period
Figure 4.15:   Response time to clear problem reports
Figure 4.16:   Cumulative problems and changes
Figure 4.17:   Count of problem reports by category
Figure 4.18:   Report of changes against time by category
Figure 4.19:   Number of products at a version number
Figure 4.20:   Rework costs
Figure 4.21:   Effectiveness of clearing problems
Figure 4.22:   Number of modules against metric value
Figure 4.23:   Size of modules
Figure 4.24:   Defects found according to size of module
Figure 4.25:   Frequency of module reuse
Figure 4.26:   Software structure
Figure 4.27:   Resource utilisation in target processor

Figure 5.1:   Computer facilities utilisation
Figure 5.2:   Staff levels
Figure 5.3:   Staff turnover
Figure 5.4:   Skills available to a project
Figure 5.5:   Resource utilisation
Figure 5.6:   How programmers spend their time
Figure 5.7:   Response times from engineering

Figure 6.1:   Lifecycle costs
Figure 6.2:   Proportion of costs in lifecycle phases
Figure 6.3:   Statistical control chart
Figure 6.4:   Defect density
Figure 6.5:   Cost of changes
Figure 6.6:   Cost to repair an error in the customer specification
Figure 6.7:   Number of changes according to phase of detection
Figure 6.8:   Cost of changes according to phase of detection
Figure 6.9:   Number of changes according to the source of error
Figure 6.10:   Cost of changes according to the source of error
Figure 6.11:   Defect rate according to the size of a module
Figure 6.12:   Defect fix times

Figure 7.1:   Time to respond to problem reports
Figure 7.2:   Duration that problems have been outstanding
Figure 7.3:   Number of problem reports outstanding
Figure 7.4:   Categories of problems reported
Figure 7.5:   Variation of problems reported over time
Figure 7.6:   Percentage of failures by system component
Figure 7.7:   Cost of changes
Figure 7.8:   Categories of rework
Figure 7.9:   Rework outstanding
Figure 7.10:   Modules handled per release

Figure 8.1:   Organisation chart in the design phase of a project
Figure 8.2:   Organisation chart in the test and integration phase of
                a project
Figure 8.3:   Example of a graphical progress report
Figure 8.4:   Primary activities to obtain visibility

Figure A1.1:   A pie chart
Figure A1.2:   100% bar chart
Figure A1.3:   Bar chart
Figure A1.4:   Column chart
Figure A1.5:   Curve graph
Figure A1.6:   Shaded curve graph
Figure A1.7:   Scatter diagram

PREFACE

Over many years I have undertaken almost every role associated with software development - programmer, designer, analyst, consultant, manager, tool developer, quality assurance, configuration manager, R&D manager (have I missed anything?). I have enjoyed every task, but I always had the suspicion that the projects I was working on could have been a lot more efficient. Of course, we undertook actions to add a little extra control here, some automation there, and we even tried to reuse some modules, but this was only dabbling at the problem. Why did so many projects still overspend? Why did so many project managers end up firefighting most of their time? In 1986, whilst performing an audit on a project that was permanently slipping, I realised what was needed - Visibility!

By Visibility I mean being able to see the real status of a project the way we can all see the status of a civil engineering construction project. As a building is erected, everyone can see what progress has been made and what needs to be done. If a problem occurs (e.g. late delivery of concrete or a crane breaking down) then the repercussions are also immediately visible and corrective action can be taken to overcome the problem. If that same Visibility could be provided to software project managers then, not only would control be better, but our understanding of the process of software development would be improved. At last we could take really effective action to improve our working practices.

Once I had seen the light, I started looking for ways to provide

Visibility of software projects. Many people had seen the same light before me and I quickly found many mechanisms to provide both me and my colleagues with the Visibility we desired. In collecting these mechanisms, I found that most sources of information had only collected together a few particular viewpoints of software projects. When I started bringing them together into a coherent structure, I found many gaps which I hope I have now filled.

This book provides you with the results of my work so that it does not have to be repeated. I have provided a structure for the different viewpoints of Visibility that should ease reference into the book. At my last count, the book contains over 80 figures. Don't panic! You will not need all of these viewpoints all of the time. This is a comprehensive set from which you can choose a few to provide you with adequate Visibility most of the time. Other viewpoints can be used when you have particular problems which need to go "under the magnifying glass".

I'm sure that this book is not complete, nor could it ever be; there will always be new ways to improve Visibility of software projects. On the other hand, I believe this book provides a comprehensive set of ideas which will help you achieve the Visibility you require and even help you to develop new viewpoints. I wish you luck.

Most of the mechanisms presented here are simple and straightforward. That is their strength. Many of the techniques may tell you what is obvious about your project. The real problem is most managers can miss "obvious" problems because they were not looking properly.

As a result of doing this work I realised that managers of software projects are not alone in lacking Visibility of what they manage so I have started research on a book to help managers in business. I hope you enjoy this book and come back for the next one too!

David P Youll

Basingstoke
Great Britain
December, 1989

1

INTRODUCTION

I hesitate to start this book with yet another statement that software projects are always going over budget and deadlines. I have read it so many times before, but it is of course a marvellous introduction to a book where, yet again, you are about to be told "there is a solution to the problem; and this time it is a real solution." OK, so what's so different about this book? Well, for a start, it does not solve any problems. The benefit of this book to you, the reader, is that it helps you to solve the problems yourself within your own special environment.

There have always been large projects, but each year we see more of them. As we develop techniques to make the manager's job easier, the problem changes e.g. we now see teams distributed across countries, the technology is changing rapidly (new tools, multi-processor solutions, new languages and computer architectures). Throughout all this, the manager has to coordinate a large team of people to complete the project on schedule within the budget. The overriding problem for managers of software projects is that they can't see what their staff are doing. On a hardware project there are early signs of progress with the creation of models and prototypes. Real progress can easily be monitored on large structures like a building or a ship as parts of the hardware are linked together. If there is a problem the manager can usually *see* it.

A software problem is quite different. Software can not be seen. Even when software components have been successfully linked, it is almost impossible for a project manager to predict whether the product is 1 week, 1 year or even 10 years from delivery. Even during the project, the manager can find software development staff unwilling to give estimates of when they will finish. "I'm going to finish this software as soon as I can; wasting time producing estimates and plans is only going to delay the whole project" is a cry most managers have come across. This lack of visibility of what is happening leads most managers into the traditional type: *the firefighter*. Firefighters spend their time rushing from one problem to another and are sometimes seen by senior managers as "very active, always solving problems; what would we do without them". This book shows that there is another, more effective approach to project management.

Firefighting managers have little control over where their projects are going and when they will finish. They are at their happiest when they have found a "fire" and are *reacting* to its consequences. There is another form of management; it is usually termed *proactive* in management handbooks. To be a proactive manager one needs clear visibility of what is happening in the project; a visibility that will enable you to predict the future!

Many software managers have long assumed that software is "invisible" and that, unlike in the hardware world, progress and achievement are hard to measure. However, recent developments in various centres across the world have changed this. This book brings together these developments, enabling software project managers to quickly adopt new techniques which will bring them immediate practical benefit.

Many practical case examples are included to ensure the readers can return to their work with immediate and practical benefits.

WHAT IS THE ROLE OF A MANAGER?

In the briefest of summaries, the role of a project manager is to ensure that a *product* (e.g. a software program) is developed, corrected or enhanced within a certain *timescale* (a project always has a beginning and an end) using the *resources* (e.g. money, staff, hardware) assigned for the purpose. The manager will assign the resources to *activities* required to produce the product and, if the resources are adequate, the project will be completed within the timescale. Unless something unexpected happens.

Since every software project is different it is impossible to predict perfectly the resources and timescales required to complete it. Every activity usually has many risks which might delay its start or completion. Hence, the role of the project manager is to use their experience in allocating resources so that they are being effective most of the time. Then, when a problem does occur, corrective action (i.e. control and reallocation of resources) can be taken swiftly and effectively.

WHY IS THERE A NEED FOR VISIBILITY?

Every software project is different; even using a different team of people to do exactly the same piece of work can have dramatic effects on costs and timescales. This simple fact is often difficult to accept when most of us have experience of the hardware world in which many projects are almost duplicates of previous work. If they are not, they are called "research". The difference is due to the nature of the work: every hardware product has to be manufactured individually and the greatest proportion of resources is assigned to the manufacturing process; each software product is manufactured only once and then copied many times with the greatest proportion of the resources occupied in the design process.

Talk of project delays and budget overruns is still common in the software industry. When these are analysed, many excuses for the delays are found, but rarely is there a major single cause. The simple fact is, major slippages often occur because of many minor problems. Individually, they and their effects are not noticed. Only after they have been accumulated over a long time do the effects "suddenly" appear. The manager who ignores these problems by making the excuse that "every one is working as hard as possible so what more can senior management want?" is only saving up problems for later firefighting.

The purpose of visibility is to help managers find out what problems are facing them each day and to predict what problems they will probably face in the future. What would they do if they knew? That could well be the topic for several more books; it is assumed here that a major step towards improving the effectiveness of a manager is to provide the information that will enable them to make timely decisions and to take effective action. The main benefits of this will be more accurate planning, anticipation of problems, better utilisation of resources and no sudden changes to project costs or timescales that would upset senior management or customers. With better information to base decisions on, a manager can be more assertive in assuming control of a project rather than react to its problems (don't forget, what you can't measure, you can't control). Managers are the key to the success of a project since, without their timely and effective controls, delays and additional costs are inevitable.

Alternatively, the information can be used as a powerful means of persuading customers or senior mangers to provide additional resources, budgets or time to complete the project or, in the worst case, to decide that the project should be halted immediately. This latter decision is one that is rarely made since, once started, managers do not like losing "face" by having their project stopped. Hence, not having full visibility of the problems their project is facing allows them to continue in the face of adversity, even when it started with inflated and unreasonable expectations.

To clarify the benefits of having visibility, a number of key questions that a manager should always have answers for are summarised below.

CRITICAL QUESTIONS FOR MANAGERS

What action must be taken NOW to ensure that the product meets requirements, especially reliability, when it is released?

Is the product going to meet its desired reliability level?
Is the Verification, Validation & Testing process thorough enough?
    How is thoroughness being measured?
What types of defects are getting through the process of Verification, Validation & Testing?
    How could they be found earlier?
    How could they be avoided?
    How much is rework costing?
        Is rework effective?
        Are there unexpected side effects to rework?
When can the product be released?
    What will it cost to maintain?
    What resources will be required for maintenance of the product?

What action must be taken NOW to achieve/improve on price/delivery date?

> What has been achieved/what has still to be done?
> What is the critical path?
> > Can any delivery dates be brought forward?
> > Can resources be reassigned to benefit?
> Are the forward plans based on realistic estimates?
> > What have the resources achieved to date?
> > Have the completed activities shown the estimates to be (in)accurate consistently?
> > Can the rate of progress be improved to meet critical objectives?
> > Have previous actions to improve the rate of progress been effective?
> What have been the problems in the project and will they continue?
> > Which activities have absorbed most resources?
> > Does an analysis of costs by component or activity type indicate any problems?
> > How much rework is occurring?
> > Why is the rework occurring?
> What impact would a change in QA or management resources have on the final costs and end date?
> > Can the change be monitored for effectiveness?

What action must be taken NOW to improve effectiveness of maintenance/support?

> Is the support improving?
> Is the product improving?
> What reliability/availability is being achieved?
> What problems are affecting the customers?
> > How many are there?
> > What are the repercussions for the customer?
> > How long are they taking to fix and at what cost?
> > How is the customer affected by a new release (e.g. cost of installation)?
> > Is corrective action effective?
> Would preventive maintenance be effective?
> > Should some components be redesigned?

What action must be taken NOW to improve competitive advantage?

> Is the process (methods/tools) of development/maintenance improving?
>> By how much/ at what benefit?
>> What product reliability can be expected from the chosen process?
>> What would be the effect of introducing new methods/tools now?
>> Which part of the process introduces the most defects, at what cost?
> Are the support facilities (e.g. computing) meeting the needs of the project?
>> How can senior management be persuaded to improve the facilities?

Project managers often think they know the answers to these questions because of the information provided to them by their staff, but they rarely have a factual basis. Sometimes managers do not wish to ask these questions in case they hear something they would rather not know about. However, although there is a cost involved in asking questions, the manager needs the information they provide in order to exercise control, both in the event of progress being bad or good.

WHAT SHOULD A PROJECT MANAGER HAVE VISIBILITY OF?

To have visibility is to have evidence which indicates the current state of the project. The state can be determined by monitoring a number of characteristics of the project and their evolution with time. Characteristics include product size, cost; number of documents and tests produced; number of reviews held.

There are a large number of characteristics that can be monitored in a project. They can be conveniently grouped under the following headings, the five "P"s:

- *Plans -*   providing visibility forward to targets in the future.

- *Progress -*   providing visibility backward to what has been achieved at what cost.

- *Product -* providing visibility of the quality of what has been created by the project.

- *Process -* providing visibility of the effectiveness of the methods and tools used on the project.

- *Peripherals -* providing visibility of the effectiveness of support activities to the project, many of which are not directly under the project manager's control e.g. computing, training, administration.

On a project where an existing product is being maintained there are additional characteristics which a manager may want to monitor. These are described under the heading of *Visibility of Maintenance*.

The characteristics of a project have interdependencies on each other so it is important that a project manager has a broad visibility across all of the above areas. It is not necessary to have full visibility of all characteristics of a project all the time. There is a cost associated with visibility so a manager must decide on the key areas where visibility is required. If these indicate a problem exists then further visibility can be obtained. The frequency at which visibility is obtained and the number of mechanisms used must be left to the project manager to decide. The decision is based on a trade off between the costs and the benefits of visibility. It will also depend on the size of the project and experience in anticipating some of the problems.

One way for a manager to decide what level of detail is required when the project is being monitored is to consider the question posed by Fred Brooks: "How does a project get to be a year late?" The answer is "One day at a time". Managers often consider in retrospect why their previous project failed to meet its deadline, but fail to come up with one underlying cause that explains everything. Brooks's answer is simple: each day that a small activity is delayed is significant. There are many activities on a project and even small delays can add up to a large total.

I was once a designer on a project where I was working hard, head down, nights and weekends, for a completion by the deadline in three weeks. It was at this time that the project manager announced to his team and the customer that the delivery date had slipped by six months. Everyone was stunned. Earlier in the project, the project manager had dropped cost monitoring in order to save costs (sic). When he bothered to investigate progress he found that slippage had occurred. Since his team was 80 strong, he discovered 40 man years had been lost. I am not recommending all managers should monitor costs so that they can account for every single day of a person's time (possibly resulting in "paralysis by analysis"!), but I do implore you not to "lose" man-years of effort. I think it was Tom De Marco who said "If you can not measure what you are doing then you have no control. All you have left is hysterical optimism." The only unforgivable failure is the failure to learn from previous failures.

As a result of obtaining visibility a project manager takes on a role similar to that of a captain on an aircraft. There are lots of indicators that the captain monitors, many of which he only monitors rarely when the key indicators suggest trouble is brewing. If the instrumentation fails when the captain is landing the plane in thick fog, then a catastrophe is bound to occur. A similar result can be expected for managers who try to control their projects without instrumentation. If they employ the techniques of visibility, managers should find themselves operating in a closed loop control situation where they have real control of the project, rather then reacting to its day to day problems on an ad-hoc basis (see figure 1.1).

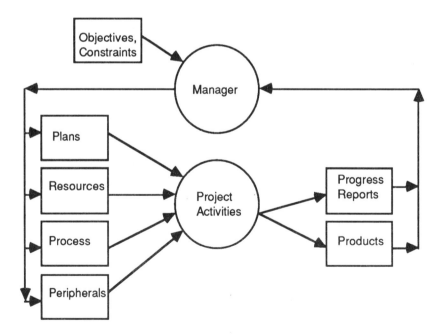

Figure 1.1: The manager in a closed loop control situation

Figure 1.2: Visibility over the project

HOW VISIBILITY IS OBTAINED

The traditional means of obtaining visibility is by preparing plans and then monitoring costs by asking the team to fill in timesheets. The information is usually presented to a project manager in the form of networks, tables of data or spreadsheets. Often the information the manager needs is hidden within reams of listings, making it a very laborious process to find. If the manager doesn't find the information, there will no doubt be someone who can point to the relevant data at a later date when the project has found itself in major trouble and say the answer was there all the time - not very helpful.

There are other ways of collecting and presenting metrics about the project which can help a manager. Rather than provide a manager with detailed analysis of each activity, the manager needs to utilise techniques which lift him or her above the action and provide a broad perspective of the project as a whole. Small problems are always being faced on a project so, without an overall picture, a manager might become entangled in them and not see more important difficulties elsewhere (see figure 1.2).

Presentation of the data is very important because there is a lot of data available and a manager does not want to spend all his time sifting through data. One of the simplest forms of presenting data quickly and effectively is in a graph. As a project progresses, many characteristics evolve and a graph can quickly inform a manager that all is going according to schedule, or not. For example, one can quickly ask "is the rate of change as expected?", "are we going to achieve that target on schedule?".

As an example, what can you read from the graph shown in figure 1.3? The graph shows only two lines: the original planned cumulative costs for the project and the actual cumulative costs to date, plotted against time.

Even a quick glance will tell you that the actual costs are below the planned spend. What is more important is that it tells a manager that actual costs are well behind plan so, assuming productivity targets have been met, major replanning of resource utilisation needs to be done immediately if the target end date is to be met on schedule. The manager can use the trend of the actual costs to review what will happen in the future. If this is combined with a review of the forecast costs to completion, a new forecast for the completion date can be produced, as shown in figure 1.4.

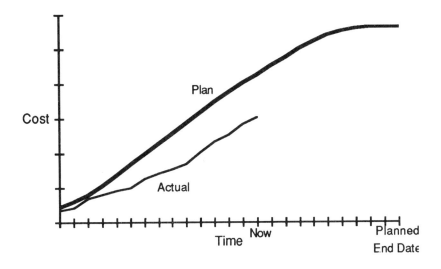

Figure 1.3: Graph showing Actual Costs and Planned Costs v. Time

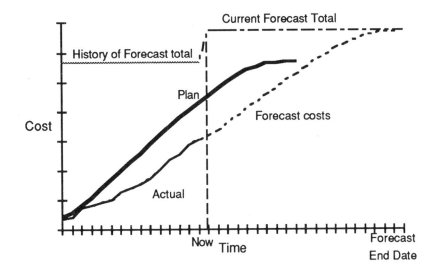

Figure 1.4: Graph showing predicted end date

If the manager is forced by the customer to stick with the original end date then, assuming costs are a good indicator of achievement, the manager will have to increase the resources used on the project.

The graph gives visibility to the difference between the current and the required rate of spend and indicate the size of the action required from the manager. If it is larger than the manager feels is possible, then the customer must be informed that a slip in schedule must be expected.

The scenario described here presents a fairly typical story, but why didn't the manager take action earlier? If action has been taken then why wasn't it effective? By analysing this graph on a regular basis the manager will gain early visibility of problems, enabling early and relatively easy actions to be taken. Even if a large problem does occur, a graph provides a manager with the ability to give an accurate estimate for a new completion date.

We've all heard the phrase "a picture is worth a thousand words" and the same is true for a graph. Consider the following:

(1)   Rather than read through tens or even hundreds of data values in a long listing, a graph can present plans, actual and forecast values, and budgets on a single chart since each value requires only one point on the page.

(2)   A time ordered sequence of values on a graph will show trends (gradients) and even changes in the trends over a number of weeks. When compared with planned trends the reader can quickly tell if the progress is inadequate and by how much. More importantly, the difference between actual trend and the trend required to complete the project on schedule indicates to a manager the degree of change required. This is very difficult to assess without a graph.

(3)   A time ordered sequence of values on a graph can be used to indicate if certain project targets (e.g. production of test specifications) are going to be achieved at the planned date. The current trend will indicate if the target is likely to be achieved and, if necessary, a new target can be quickly calculated.

(4)   Graphs are an excellent way to summarise data in order to detect patterns or to identify points, at a glance, which are outside of the general trend.

Other useful techniques for presenting snapshots of a project quickly are histograms and pie charts. Examples of these will be given in the later chapters and the Appendix.

I have used graphs of various metrics for several years now to provide me with more visibility of the work I and my staff are doing. The major benefits are that they give a concise summary of the state of a project and management attention is directed towards what actions need to be taken to correct any problems. Written progress reports which go into detail on what has been happening in the past are no longer created. What matters is the present and its impact on the future.

A question going through the readers mind may be "Visibility is all very well, but what about the costs of obtaining it?" The short answer is "Read on", because many of the techniques are very simple and the increasing automation of software development is enabling many of the techniques to be automated. Another answer could be "What is the cost of not having visibility?", but the reader should probably answer this question after reading the rest of the book.

STRUCTURE OF THIS BOOK

I do not claim that this book is a complete guide to the techniques for obtaining visibility. I have brought together a number of techniques and put them into a structure which I hope is useful. I am sure many of the techniques can be used to practical benefit, but I do urge the reader to use this book as a spur to analysing the problems on their own project and to develop techniques to improve visibility of their own specific problems.

Most of the examples presented are simple and straightforward to use. More complex analysis of projects can be done using metrics which require some statistical knowledge. However, do be aware that statistics can be used to prove almost anything if used by the unwary.

A quick summary of the contents of this book is:

Chapter 2 contains a review of the techniques to obtain *forward visibility*. These techniques are used throughout a project since the purpose of obtaining visibility is to enable plans to be updated with the latest information.

Chapter 3 contains a review of the techniques which can be used to analyse *progress* and to identify what progress can be achieved in the future.

Chapter 4 provides a review of the visibility that can be obtained on the *quality* of the product.

Chapter 5 looks at the *support* provided to a project manager in the form of computer services, quality assurance, recruitment, etc.

Chapter 6 contains techniques for gaining visibility of the *process* of software development.

Chapter 7 contains techniques for analysing the effectiveness of projects which are *maintaining* operational software.

Chapter 8 looks into the practical aspects of *achieving visibility*, including costs and identification of the key variables to be monitored.

The Appendix provides a summary of the uses that can be made of graphs when analysing data.

The book contains many examples of graphs that can be used on software projects. In reviewing these examples the reader should note that:

All graphs are derived from hypothetical data. However, the data is chosen to be typical of what may be found on real projects and are for illustrative purposes only.

Scale values are normally omitted. Scale values serve only to identify the magnitude of the data, which is not important for the purposes here. Scale values will naturally be used in practice, but their omission does not detract from the message provided by each graph. A graph is presented to study relationships, not to identify specific data. If accuracy of data, or specific values, are required, then the graph should be supported by these separately.

Several graphical styles are used to present the data. The Appendix provides some guidelines as to which style is best for particular data, but the examples given in the main text do not always follow the guidelines precisely. My purpose in doing this is to provide the reader with many examples of the variety of styles that can be used to present data.

2

FORWARD VISIBILITY

INTRODUCTION

The whole purpose of visibility is to increase the probability that we are taking the right action today to achieve our targets in the future. Planning is the first action we must perform on a project and it gives us our first view of the future. A plan provides a schedule of activities and events which together achieve a goal. However, a plan is based on estimates of the size and duration of activities, and estimates are based on probabilities. As each week of the project passes, some of our estimates will mature with sometimes better and sometimes worse results than expected. Each result can have an impact on our outstanding estimates and we may wish to alter them and create a new plan.

Without a plan, a project manager can not control a project because there is nothing to measure achievement against. The later chapters in this book show how visibility of progress and other factors will help to shape our view of the future and require alteration of the plans. The frequency at which plans should be updated is considered in Chapter 3.

Many projects start, and even end without a plan - why? A plan is simply a mechanism to allow its author to identify and schedule activities according to constraints and priorities. Anyone managing a project without a plan, simply reacts to *what appears to be* the current most important project activity. If the manager is always doing something that is very important then he can't go wrong - right?! This is the strategy taken by people who like to fight fires.

Some important issues for a manager who acts like a fireman to consider are:

*   How can you be sure that you are performing the most important task if you have not produced a plan?

*   Spending time tackling the biggest priority activity is important, but are the right resources assigned to it?

*   Are the remaining resources assigned appropriately to the next most urgent activities?

*   When an activity is completed, which is the most important to be started next?

The production of a plan will help to resolve these issues because a plan provides the project team, the manager and the customer with forward visibility of what must be done today, tomorrow, next week, etc. until the end of the project. For example, a plan should show:

*   What has to be done (the activities) and the best order in which to perform the activities.

*   A schedule of activities which makes the best use of resources available (hardware and manpower) within the constraints of the project.

*   Potential problems ahead, enabling the manager to initiate preemptive action.

*   Short term, clear targets which motivate staff much better than long term, vague targets.

*   The costs of completing the project in terms of staff numbers, skills and other resource utilisation.

*   The expected completion date.

- When and where resources are needed, and when they can be released. Since effective utilisation of resources is required to achieve project budgets and deadlines, this type of visibility can be of great assistance to project managers when they are trying to meet budget constraints.

With clear visibility of what has to be achieved, the project manager can make firm decisions about recruitment and when to purchase equipment. In addition, it gives the manager clear factual evidence when it is necessary to return to senior management, sales staff, or a customer in order to persuade them to alter timescales and/or budgets for the project. Once the project is running, progress can be measured and compared against the plans to obtain early visibility of problems occurring.

The very first plan will, of course, be based on experience and estimates which include a lot of guesswork, but you have to start from somewhere. As the project progresses, feedback on the original estimates will permit the accuracy of our forward visibility to be increased with better plans. If you don't start to plan in the first place, then you will never gain this feedback and learn from experience.

It is sometimes argued that a plan is unnecessary because the tasks are short, simple and obvious. However, as soon as several people are involved over a period the interdependency between tasks becomes so large that the benefits of a plan outweigh the costs of developing it. It is commendable that staff wish to be performing useful work, but their management need reliable estimates of costs and end dates so that they can anticipate the repercussions of customer requirements not being met.

Too often projects fail due to the setting of unrealistic budgets and targets for completion. A good plan can provide concrete evidence for a project manager to persuade his/her senior management that the project is infeasible right from the start. If the project does receive the go ahead then the plan forms the basis for controlling the project i.e. it provides:

- guidance on how the project is progressing - lack of progress deserves management attention;

- guidance on when resources will be needed, enabling them to be ordered well in advance.

THE ELEMENTS OF A PLAN

A plan specifies a valid time schedule for *activities* which are performed by *resources* within the *constraints on resources* and *events* imposed on the project.

Activities

An activity is a package of work with clear, defined goals. It should also have clearly defined quality metrics which define when the activity can be recorded and agreed as complete. In order to schedule and analyse a plan, the following attributes need to be defined for each activity:

(1) *Constraints on the start date.* An activity's start date may be constrained by an event and/or completion of other activities.

(2) *Constraints on the completion date.* An activity may be constrained to finish by a particular date in order to, say, provide a deliverable for the contract.

(3) *Estimated Duration.* The expected duration of the activity must be defined. This must not be the most optimistic duration, but an average which allows for the activity to be performed quickly if there are no problems and the best staff are assigned, or slowly if there are problems or there are only inexperienced staff available to do the work.

(4) *Estimated cost/budget.* For more sophisticated analysis the probable cost and even a range of estimated minimum to maximum costs of the activity can be defined.

(5) *Resource assignments.* These can be in the form of general resources (e.g. persons, skill types or hardware) for defined periods, and/or specific assignments of individuals or other resources for periods (e.g. F Smith for 2 weeks).

(6) *Category.* The validity of a plan can be analysed by studying the allocation of resources to different *types* of activity (e.g. management, production, QA) and in different *phases* (e.g. design or testing) of the work programme.

(7) *Product.* If there is no clearly defined, measurable product to be produced as the result of an activity, the activity will be treated like a "slush fund", i.e. all sorts of related work will be recorded as part of this activity rather than as part of other, tightly specified activities. Hence, whenever possible, each activity should have a specification for the product to be produced plus quality measures/tests which define when the product is complete. This may seem a great chore when many small activities have to be defined, but the specifications don't have to be long and the lack of a specification can lead to the wrong work being done.

There is no simple definition of the scope of an activity. They can be as small or as large as the planner wishes. A common mechanism for planners to use is to start off by identifying the major activities and then to break each of these into smaller activities. The process can be repeated as necessary until an appropriate level of detail is specified. This results in the creation of an hierarchy of activities which is sometimes referred to as a Work Breakdown Structure (WBS - see figure 2.2).

Resources

The activities of a plan can not be performed without resources and often they require some combination of resources to achieve their goals. Sometimes a manager will only consider the manpower resource when planning. However, the availability of hardware, accommodation, techniques and tools are also important resources that contribute to the success of a project and they need to be considered in a plan.
    Depending on the level of detail and the analysis required, resources can be described in general terms (e.g. 2 people, 2 analysts, 3 one MIP workstations) or specific terms (e.g. J Jones, Vax 11-780 number 5). The more information that is provided, the more comprehensive an analysis of the plans, to identify resource overloads, can be.

Resource Constraints

Constraints restrict the availability of resources (people and hardware) in certain periods (e.g. 20 staff in November, 40 hours per week from J Jones). Analysis will be required to check in advance that these constraints will not be broken during the project.

Events

Some activities cannot start before certain events occur (e.g. the delivery of a CPU), whilst others must finish before the event can occur (e.g. a customer must have the installation during the Christmas closedown of the plant).

ESTIMATING

Estimating for software projects is the subject for a whole book, and there are several available. Hence, in this section I just want to highlight a few factors that affect how estimates are used on projects.

Accurate estimates are needed in order to confirm the project will provide a real cost benefit, to establish realistic budgets and to enable managers to control the project against a plan. An estimate is not a guess; estimates take time and judgment in order to be accurate. Wild guesses or non-estimates (e.g. quoting a new estimate as the last estimate plus permissible slip) will not produce effective plans and will negate most of the attempts to gain effective control.

The actual cost of activities will depend greatly on the skills of the person who actually does the work. The estimates and the accuracy assigned to them must reflect the variety of skills available; it must not be assumed that an expert will perform every task.

The accuracy of estimating can be greatly increased by providing planners with visibility of what happened on previous projects, as well as providing them with an analysis, based on progress to date, of how well they have planned on their current project. This topic will be covered in the next chapter. Much experience is also available in books and there is support from tools for estimating.

Although accuracy in estimating will improve visibility, it is not necessary to demand high accuracy for all planning purposes. For example, rough estimates on a "macro" scale will be adequate for initial budgeting and feasibility analysis. Once a project is running, only the current phase of work may need to be planned in detail. The manager must choose the accuracy required to achieve the desired level of forward visibility.

Most project managers have come across the problem that "my boss will not accept my estimates because they are too high for the customer." Rather than allow senior management to risk projects based on their own judgment, estimators should provide their management with visibility of their estimating procedures. Too many projects start through inflated and unreasonable expectations of the customer so it is no wonder they fail. On the other hand, an unreasonably high estimate can lose business. Senior managers must be taught that estimating is a skill and that estimates are based on practical experience rather than hunches.

Specifying the activities required for a project, together with their attributes, is not an easy process. Just identifying the need for an activity is a process requiring years of experience, as demonstrated on many projects where overruns can be directly put down to staff performing unplanned (but not unnecessary) activities, e.g. quality reviews and inspections, rework after review, user guidelines. Such unplanned activities may not be project related; for example, training, holidays, sickness, writing a proposal for another project or the repercussions of hardware failure or maintenance.

Estimating should be performed independently of the setting of fixed targets, deadlines or budgets. For example, if the estimated end date falls on the wrong side of a deadline then either the deadline should be put back or the work must be reduced. Even when an estimate matches the deadline, there is still a problem for the project manager because it means that there is a 50% probability of the project overrunning. Hence, in order to have a high probability of meeting a fixed deadline, the estimated duration must come within the deadline by an amount which at least equals the estimating accuracy. The same is true if the project must come within budget (see figure 2.1).

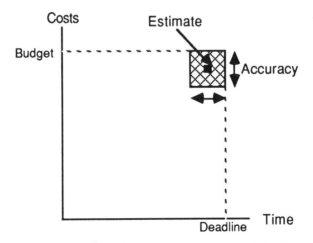

Figure 2.1: Estimate compared to budget and deadline

Software development is about designing solutions to problems. Thus, since the time it will take to solve the problem is normally difficult to predict, estimates at the early stages in a software project are likely to have poor accuracy. Methods and tools are available to assist the estimator, but there is nothing better than receiving feedback during the project and using this to produce better estimates. Examples of estimating techniques are (*Software Engineering Economics*, 1981 by Boehm provides a good introduction to this topic):

• Use a model which relates cost, size, duration and other factors in an equation.

• Use experience and analogies with similar projects.

• Compare top-down estimates with the accumulated bottom-up estimates.

The best advice is never use only one estimating technique, but compare the results of several. Once you have understood the differences between the results and learned the strengths and weaknesses of each technique you will be able to come up with a reasonable estimate. It will also be possible for you to start building your own estimating model, based on your own projects. This will reflect your own development environment and the features of projects you deal with most frequently.

Don't forget your estimate is not complete until you have defined its accuracy, i.e. its range of acceptable deviation. This is an important factor during the project to stop any overreaction if the estimate is not being achieved.

CONTINGENCY AND MINIMISING RISK

Every estimate involves a risk, but some have greater impact than others. A plan is not complete without consideration of the risks and ways of minimising their impact by preparing contingency plans. Whereas completing an activity ahead of schedule will have minimal impact on a project, a major delay in one activity can have disastrous impact if it is not foreseen and contingency plans implemented quickly. The greatest risk on a project is with items which are outside of the project managers control, e.g. the delivery of hardware from a supplier.

Such items should not be put on the critical path and/or some penalty arrangement should be put in the supplier's contract to increase their motivation to achieve their deadline.

Examples of the types of risks that a planner must take into account are:

- Hardware or support may have unexpected problems, especially if it is a new model.

- The customer requirements may include unexpected inconsistencies which take time to resolve.

- Key project staff may leave.

- Novel applications may contain unexpected pitfalls.

- External suppliers may not meet their planned delivery dates.

- Appropriate numbers of staff with relevant experience may not be available.

If you're not careful, you could spend the whole project planning for all the eventualities and do no work! As with most management activities, a balance has to be struck between the costs of preparing a plan with contingencies and the risk of a problem occurring without contingency for it.

TARGETS

Part of a plan must be the specification of *targets,* e.g. rate of production of test cases, total test cases to be produced, rate of finding faults, total faults expected to be found. Targets help the team to understand what it is they are expected to achieve, thus increasing motivation. Targets must be achievable and setting them with the help of the project staff will increase their motivation further.

Most of the measures presented in this book require a target to be set. Hence, target setting for each of the measures a manager wishes to utilise should be a major part of the planning process. Targets are also an important part of the estimating process since they form the basis on which many estimates are made.

WORK BREAKDOWN STRUCTURES

On a large project, the manager will not be able to specify every detailed activity immediately. The process of developing a plan often identifies large items of work initially and then breaks these down into more detail. The result can be displayed in the form of a Work Breakdown Structure (WBS - see figure 2.2).

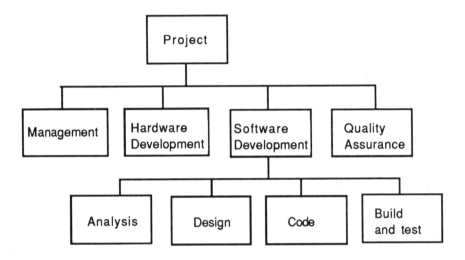

Figure 2.2: Work Breakdown Structure

A WBS provides staff with visibility of the tasks to be done and how the items of work fit in to the overall project. During the project it is relatively easy to accumulate costs into the tasks identified in the WBS. This can provide useful information when planning future projects because it can show the proportion of work spent in various categories of tasks (e.g. design, coding, etc.).

ANALYSIS OF PLANS

Having specified the attributes of all the activities on a project, visibility of their interdependencies can be provided by drawing a time ordered network of the activities. The most common format used is that of the PERT network (see figure 2.3). In the example shown, each activity is represented by a circle and time dependencies between activities are represented by the connecting lines. The number displayed in each circle is the expected duration in weeks of each activity.

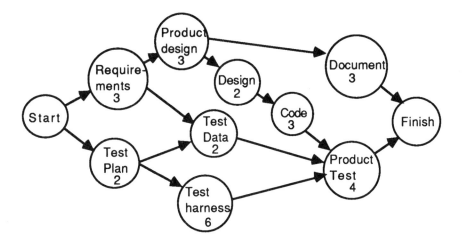

Figure 2.3: A PERT network

Notes 2.3: This network shows that the coding takes 2 weeks, it cannot start before the design is complete, and the product test can not start before the code is complete. It also shows that, if resources are available, a test harness could be developed in parallel with the creation of the test data.

The term PERT is an acronym for Programme Evaluation and Review Technique. PERT charts were developed and first used by the Lockheed Corporation and the U.S. Navy for the development of the Polaris missile programme in the late 1950s.

A simple addition of the durations of activities for each path through the PERT network will identify the path that is longest (sometimes there is more than one) and hence the critical activities which will constrain the earliest completion date of the project. The sequence of these activities forms the critical path(s) through the network (see figure 2.4). In the example shown, the critical path is highlighted and the two numbers to the side of each activity represent the earliest start and earliest finish week of each activity. An analysis can also be performed to determine the latest possible start and finish weeks of an activity. The difference between earliest and latest start shows the freedom available when scheduling resources.

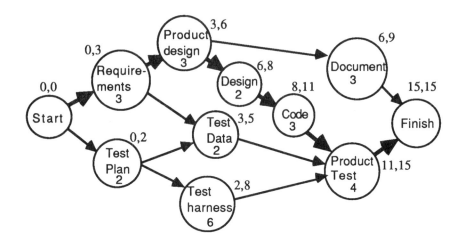

Figure 2.4: Network showing critical path

Notes 2.4: Beware of concentrating management efforts on ensuring the activities on the critical path are achieved on schedule. All of the durations in the plan are estimates which may turn out too high or low in practice. Hence, other paths through the network may become the critical path during the project. A manager can use some of the more recent analysis tools to analyse the plans to find out which paths, given the accuracy of the estimates, might become critical during the project.

One factor which will stop a project meeting its objectives is the availability of resources; they just can't be turned on and off as desired. An analysis of the resources required by a plan, together with a knowledge of the expected availability of resources (see figure 2.5), will probably require the project manager to review the network of activities. By changing start dates, durations and assignments, the resource requirements can be scheduled to meet availability and permit individuals to move smoothly from one activity to another with no overloading.

The resource analysis can be done by hand, but automated analysis, especially when tasks are frequently rescheduled, is a real help. The tools can also take many other factors into consideration, for example, the effect of long lasting activities (e.g. management, quality assurance) which have little impact on the logic of a PERT network.

I have seen several projects fail for the lack of this simple analysis - please do it on your projects!

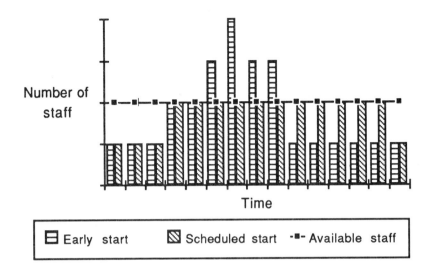

Figure 2.5: Resources required for a project

Notes 2.5: This resource profile is a simple profile for a project requiring only a few staff over a relatively short period. It shows that if all the activities could start at their earliest possible dates a maximum of eight people would be required on the project. However, if the activities are scheduled so that a maximum of only four people are required, the project will still complete on schedule. Such a convenient conclusion is unusual.

When larger numbers of staff are required on a project, other factors come into consideration for scheduling. For example, large numbers of staff are not available instantaneously and staff can not be put on to some work without special training. Several researchers have studied this problem and found that staff profiles on projects tend to follow a curve like that shown in figure 2.6. Any attempts to improve project timescales by following a different staff profile are likely to have significant cost impact.

Large staff numbers also creates a problem for management because it naturally leads to large communications overheads on the project. The problem grows exponentially with the size of the team and becomes a major issue for management to handle. If you must have a large team, do not forget to take this factor into account when making estimates.

Another factor to take into account when scheduling resources is the skills required. For example, if you have only one skilled analyst available then you may find that availability to do critical tasks may define your critical path on the project. Availability of staff resources is discussed further in Chapter 5.

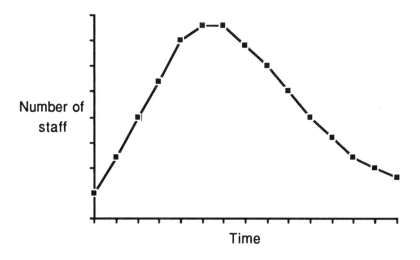

Figure 2.6: Typical profile of resources used on a project

Factors to consider when scheduling activities are:

(1) *The number of activities that can be performed in parallel.* The number of concurrent activities is limited by the resources available at that time. Does the project manager know what resources are expected to be available during the project? The assignments of specific resources (e.g. skills) also limit the activities that can be performed in parallel. Note that individuals can not easily chop and change between activities simply to meet the demands of a schedule.

(2) *Risks.* Many things can go wrong, and many problems might occur. The best schedule makes allowance for these factors in order to minimise their potential impact. The provision of alternative schedules (contingency plans) is another way of dealing with this situation.

(3) *The elapsed time of activities.* Resources will not be available for periods in the project due to unpredictable causes e.g. sickness, holidays, mechanical breakdown and external project activities (recruitment, proposal writing, etc.) Although specific dates for such events can be predicted, a level of resource non-availability must be planned in over long periods.

(4) *Bottlenecks.* Sometimes certain activities will have a major impact on the plan. When these are identified the manager can try to alter the plans to reduce or remove their impact.

(5) *Reducing timescales increases cost.* If a manager wishes to reduce the project timescales then costs are increased due to increased recruitment, increased management overheads, increased inter-project communications, etc. Although this may be countered by cost saving to the customer through early delivery of the product, the manager must be aware that the risk of failure is increased since even small delays can be very costly.

(6) *Resource planning should include hardware.* The scheduling of use of hardware, accommodation, techniques and tools, supplies (e.g. paper, stationary), communications lines, etc. are just as important to the project as the availability of manpower.

The increasing availability of computer tools for analysing plans has greatly improved the effectiveness of a planner. This has been an important development because scheduling is not easy when there are many variables, trade offs and risks to consider. And the project manager usually wants advice immediately so that idle resources can be effectively utilised!

Scheduling is a great aid to a manager's forward visibility because the resultant schedule will indicate:

• The minimum time it will take to complete the project and the activities which constrain this time (the critical path).

ə The resources required during the project.

• The expected end date of the project.

• The expected cost of the project.

This is the minimum information the manager should expect to work with. Additional information can be found using tools which, given the minimum, maximum and expected durations and costs for each activity, can predict the minimum, maximum and expected project end date and final cost.

As a result of analysing the schedule, the manager will normally have to add constraints to the network to reflect the availability of staff. This will no doubt cause more paths to be just subcritical. This is normal and sets the scene for the manager's key role during the project - balancing the available resources against the most important work to be done. Every time the availability of resources changes or activities complete later than estimated the manager should review the plans for the repercussions.

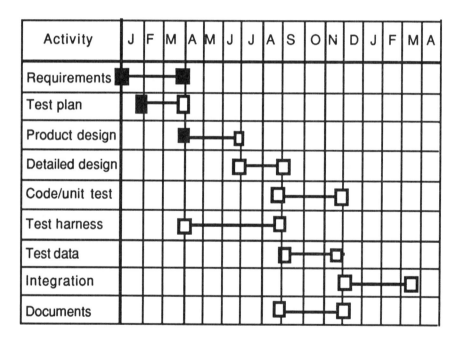

Figure 2.7: A Gantt chart

Notes 2.7: Activities are listed down the left hand side of the chart and time is measured from left to right. In this example, time is plotted in calendar months. The boxes signify the start or end date of an activity, with connecting lines showing the duration. Dependencies between activities are not shown. The Gantt chart can be used to show progress by filling in the appropriate boxes where an activity has started or finished. The use of Gantt charts to monitor progress against plans is discussed further in the next Chapter.

If he's not careful, a project manager can end up continuously replanning. The way out of this situation is to use modern planning tools and to include contingencies in the plan so that minor changes can be absorbed without the need to replan.

A PERT network assists the scheduling of activities, but it is not the most convenient format for presenting to the staff the sequence of activities and their personal assignments. For these a Gantt chart is often used. A Gantt chart shows how activities are sequenced with time (see figure 2.7) and is therefore very effective for displaying a schedule of activities to the staff.

Activity	J	F	M	A	M	J	J	A	S	O	N	D	J	F	M	A
Requirements	1	1	1													
Test plan		.5	.5													
Product design				3	4	5										
Detailed design							6	6								
Code/unit test								3	6	5	4	2				
Test harness				1	1	1	2	1								
Test data									3	2	1					
Integration												5	5	4	2	
Documents									2	3	3	1				
TOTAL	1	1.5	1.5	4	5	6	8	10	11	10	8	8	5	4	2	

Figure 2.8: A personnel plan

Notes 2.8: The numbers in the boxes show the number of man months each activity requires in each month. Hence, for example, a team of 4 people is required for this project during April. The Gantt chart does not show the same information as PERT charts (e.g. dependencies are missing) so should be used in conjunction with a PERT.

One objective of the scheduling process is to provide the project manager with visibility of the ideal set of resources that would be

required to achieve his objectives, thus giving him more confidence
when he has to persuade his management to release them. Visibility
of the resources required can be provided using an alternative form of a
Gantt chart where the manpower requirements for each activity are
shown (see figure 2.8). Of course, planning and scheduling do not stop
here. One can go further to draw a Gantt chart schedule for every
member of staff so that they have clear visibility of their work over
the coming months. When planning down to this level of detail, it is
very important not to forget to include time for rework, holidays,
sickness, etc. in the schedule.

The chart shown in figure 2.8 shows a typical level of detail that
managers finish their planning at. However, even this chart leaves
many questions unanswered. Consider whether the manager concerned
has enough forward visibility to answer the following questions:

(1)   What skills are required by each activity? Can the skills be
      provided at the times required?

(2)   What does 0.5 of a person mean? Is it 1 person half-time for one
      month, or 1 person full-time for 2 weeks?

(3)   What hardware resources are required at what times?

(4)   Has rework been planned in? When are the review milestones?
      A manager should not plan for every activity to succeed because
      rework will be frequently required.

(5)   What would happen if an activity finished early? If the
      manager can not take advantage of an activity finishing early
      then the project is bound to miss its deadlines.

(6)   Is contingency planned in?

(7)   Is time allowed for new staff to read in to the project?

Obtaining answers to these questions requires effort from the project
manager at the start of a project, just when the manager is keen to be
starting "real" work. Sometimes planning can be a tedious and
frustrating process, but without the visibility it provides, the manager
is putting the project at great risk that there will be unexpected
problems ahead.

ORGANISATION VISIBILITY

Although the scheduling of resources is a key activity for the project manager, it is important to consider how the resources are to be organised and managed. An organisation chart showing the roles and responsibilities of staff should be made visible to the project team (see figure 2.9). It should be supported by Job Specifications for the key people so that their is no confusion over who is responsible for all project activities and to ensure there are no gaps.

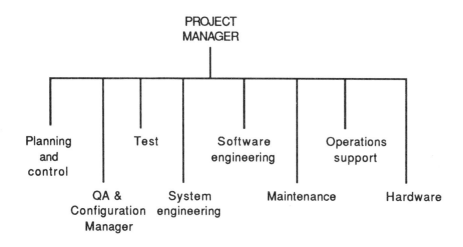

Figure 2.9: An organisation chart

Another type of chart to draw for an organisation shows how information flows through the organisation and who the decision makers are. The chart can get very complex if several roles are described so it is often appropriate just to draw one diagram for each role, with data flows shown as lines into or away from the person (see figure 2.10).

When we did this for a company I worked for, we found that there was one level of management at which many of the decisions were being made, but these managers were not receiving the information that their senior managers had. When this was made visible it became fairly obvious that the current organisation was inefficient and changes needed to be made to it. The topic of which organisation is best for a project is discussed further in Chapter 8 "Implementing Visibility."

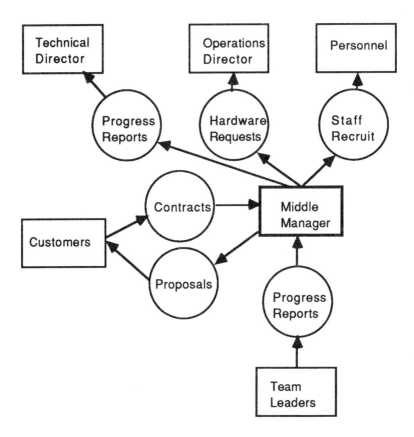

Figure 2.10: Information flow in an organisation

PLANNING TO ACHIEVE QUALITY TARGETS

The customer for a product development will have in mind some criteria for deciding whether the product meets acceptable quality levels. These quality levels are often subjective, but the project manager must define measurable objectives for quality in order that quality can be built in and controlled during the project. Quality objectives might include: fault rate of the operational system, performance characteristics, documentation quality, duration of user staff training.

With these objectives in mind, the project manager should create a quality plan. This will define the strategy and techniques to be used throughout the product development to achieve the desired quality. Techniques will be defined for avoiding defects during the development, checking to ensure no defects have crept into the product, and sometimes for even including fault tolerant mechanisms in the software. It is not the purpose of this book to define the contents of a quality plan, but some measures of quality and techniques for monitoring their achievement are presented in Chapter 4.

Having defined the quality objectives and the means for achieving them, the manager can start planning the activities on the project. If the quality levels are to be achieved then every single activity must have a clear specification of what is to be produced by the activity and the quality controls to be applied. I know this can be a long laborious process which managers find boring - I certainly do. However, the cost to specify and plan an activity is small compared to the activity cost. Without these specifications the team might relax quality when they are finding it difficult to achieve deadlines.

Another use of activity specifications is to aid communication from manager to team members. They set clear targets and reduce the possibility of staff making incorrect assumptions about what is required and doing the wrong work.

STRATEGY FOR PLANNING

Too often a plan is created to reflect target dates of "political" importance. The person who sets the target is mindless of resource constraints, justifying the target on the basis of the benefits to be obtained if the target is achieved. If proper planning is not performed then staff can become involved in working overtime to meet impossible targets. If the target is missed then everyone loses. Thorough analysis of the plans will highlight the costs and risks involved so that proper business decision making can occur. Note that a plan without any contingency will fail. Management know that some activities can be done quickly, but to bank on many activities being completed quickly is pure foolhardiness.

The preparation of a good plan takes time. One can go to very fine detail and consider all sorts of possibilities, most of which will not occur in practice. Hence, one must avoid the pitfall of over planning and produce a plan which will have the least possibility of failure and can be used to allocate resources effectively.

Another reason for not over planning is that one can never predict the future with any accuracy. We can estimate the size and duration of activities, but it is difficult to achieve high accuracy and there are always unexpected events. Also, we can never be sure that events outside our control (e.g. delivery of hardware, recruitment of staff) will occur on schedule. However, the detail of the plans will define the detail available when we require forward visibility and when we look at visibility of progress.

The decision on the level of detail will depend on the size and complexity of the project and must, in the end, rest with the project manager's experience. It is possible, and often appropriate, to plan with greater detail for the near future (say, 3 to 6 months) and with less detail for the longer term. Whatever approach is taken, it is most important that the plans cover the whole project to the very end if the scheduling and analysis process is to be effective.

Some activities are long lasting and can be very difficult to break down into sub activities. For example, an activity could be "produce 1000 sets of test data in 20 weeks." The visibility of this activity will be much improved if it has its own production plan (for example, see figures 2.11 and 2.12).

Such plans not only assist the management, but more clearly define the task set upon the team, thus increasing their motivation to achieve. Activities where this approach can be considered are production of documents, source code, tests, executed tests, fault reporting or rework on documents.

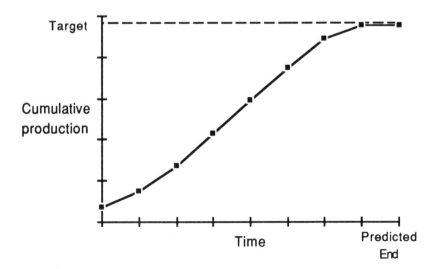

Figure 2.11: Production plan

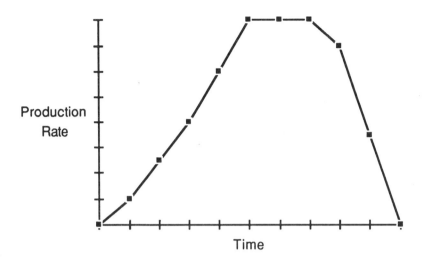

Figure 2.12: Planned rate of production

It is very important to decide in advance which aspects of the project the manager wishes to have visibility of. For example, contingency and rework are often hidden in almost every activity; should they be treated as activities to be monitored separately? Contingency is very important to a manager because it is a measure of what is unknown. On the one hand, the manager must expect the unexpected and make allowances for it. However, creating too large a contingency may make the project unprofitable so a balance of the risks and benefits has to be struck.

Rework is also very important to make visible by monitoring it separately because it is nugatory work. If it can be measured then something can be done to reduce it, thus increasing the overall staff productivity.

A common mistake when making plans is to always assume that work will be done properly. For example, when a person is given 10 days to produce a specification then it is not unusual for that person to assume that when they deliver the specification on the tenth day, the activity is finished. But which activity supports the costs of performing a quality review? If the review identifies the document as being incomplete, then which activity supports the costs of the rework? Who will do the rework? Unplanned rework will result in extra costs and delay to subsequent activities. In order for a plan not to fail because of unexpected rework, a manager must plan in activities for quality review and rework for all activities. Alternatively, budgets for all quality checks and all rework can be created, but this mechanism makes it difficult to monitor the delays between activities.

It is important to have accurate plans because the project manager will need them if he finds it necessary to go to the customer or senior management to request a change in deadlines or resources assigned. Continuing with vague plans in the hope that, with hard work and a bit of luck, the project will be completed on schedule will only lead to a demoralised team and worse problems in the future.

Planning is an iterative process because there are a large number of interacting variables and first assumptions can prove incorrect. Even when a feasible plan is produced which shows achievement of the deadline within budget, it may be possible to reschedule activities in order to reduce costs. The project manager should also bear in mind that there are often trade offs that can be made between costs and schedules. For example, the earlier that the system can be delivered the greater the benefit to the customer, but the cost of production is greater due to the overheads of large teams. Alternatively, by allowing more time for the development there will be less project overheads and lower risk of failure, but the customer will not obtain the benefits of the system until a later date. Hence, there is often an optimum duration for a project (see figure 2.13) which balances these issues. When a customer is provided visibility of the issues involved he may well alter an imposed deadline, to the relief of the manager.

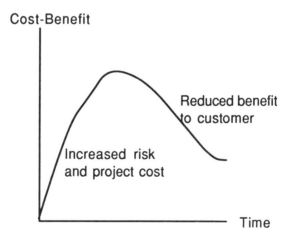

Figure 2.13: Cost - schedule trade offs

As the project progresses, the manager will gain visibility of how accurate the initial activities were planned. There are bound to be changes to the plans as the result of this experience and, during the life of a project, there will be a need to perform replanning on several occasions. However, a change in the publicised plans can lead to confusion in the team and lost motivation if it happens too frequently. People like to work to fixed targets. Hence, the project manager must choose carefully when to issue new project plans so that he and the team have clear visibility of their long term goals, whilst keeping staff motivated to achieve short term deadlines.

BENEFITS AND VISIBILITY PROVIDED BY PLANS

A well thought out, analysed plan will provide a project manager and the team with a schedule of activities together with:

* viable completion dates;

* manpower requirements during the project;

* production targets;

* computing facilities required;

* supplies, etc.

This information can be used to discuss with the project's customer the date and cost of the product at delivery. Although the customer may have firm ideas about the delivery dates and cost, the detailed analysis provided by the plan may help to persuade the customer that the requirements are not feasible within the given constraints, e.g. budget. Alternatively, the plan can be used to persuade the customer, or the manager of the project manager, that certain constraints (e.g. the availability of staff) are having a serious impact and their help is required to alleviate the situation. Managers of project managers are used to the demands from a project for extra resources so they often say "no" from instinct. A plan showing the effect of easing resource constraints will permit a more factual argument which is difficult to refuse.

The primary use of plans is in the control of the project. Progress can be monitored against them, prompting management action when progress is not consistent with the plan (see next chapter). The plans also form the basis for staff recruitment and hardware procurement, as well as providing guidance for setting up an organisation structure and initiating training courses.

Planning will not be a perfect predictor of the future and there will come a time when replanning is necessary. With a good plan as the basis for replanning, the repercussions of changes to the organisation, activities, constraints, etc. can be quantified, making a change easier to justify to the customer or in company management. This is discussed in more detail in the next chapter.

3

VISIBILITY OF PROGRESS

INTRODUCTION

On large projects, a great many deviations from the plan happen during the project. Some activities come in over their estimate, whilst others come in under. Key people are promoted, take time off for sickness, or simply leave the company. Recruitment of staff can be slower or faster than expected; suppliers delay their deliveries; or customers change their mind. With all these factors occurring, how can a project manager tell if progress is reasonable?

If a project is overspending, the project manager must be able to identify clearly whether this is due to difficult work, poor quality staff, rework due to the customer changing their mind, or staff not being utilised properly. Alternatively if the project is making faster progress than expected, this could be due to poor quality control rather than high staff productivity.

If a project manager is to have effective control of the project then visibility of progress is crucial. Some of the key questions a manager needs to answer are:

- How much work has been completed?

- How much of the project plan has been achieved?

- How much work is left to do?

- Does the achievement to date indicate poor progress and a possible need to replan the future?

In order that some visibility of progress can be obtained the following are required:

(a)   a plan;

(b)   monitoring of the start and end date of each activity;

(c)   monitoring of resources used on each activity;

(d)   monitoring of the products produced by the project activities e.g. documents, modules.

Progress can be made visible by the analysis of this data in the following forms:

- Compare progress achieved in the last period (e.g. a week or a month) against that in previous periods.

- Compare achievement to date with what is left to do.

- Review the accuracy of the estimates and predict what can be expected in the future.

- Review what the resources have been assigned to.

- Review the rate of production and the turnaround time of activities and decide if they are adequate to achieve project objectives.

This information will permit the manager to identify problems as they arise and give valuable feedback on the current accuracy of the forward plans. Depending on the information obtained, the manager may have to take action to ensure future objectives are achieved. But which action, when and how big? These are the real questions that visibility helps to answer. Mechanisms for achieving this visibility are described in more detail below.

PROGRESS VISIBILITY BY MONITORING THE UTILISATION OF RESOURCES

Slip Charts

The most common way that progress is monitored today is by the use of "slip charts". These are generally based on Gantt charts and simply involve drawing a line through the chart to show the approximate progress through activities at a given date (see figure 3.1). The same chart can be used to monitor the progress over several weeks or even months, though the lines of progress should be drawn in different colours to avoid confusion.

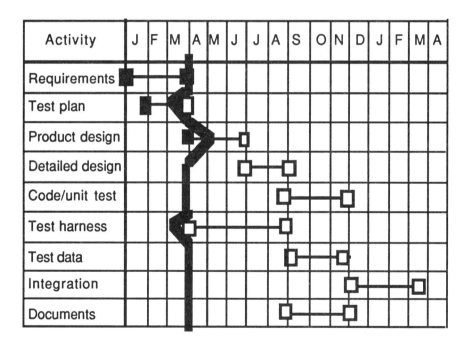

Figure 3.1: Slip chart

This is the simplest method I know of displaying progress, so long as you have spent the time creating a plan in the first place. It is strongly recommended and, when the slip lines become too "wavy", it is a good indicator of when the plans need to be redrawn.

One problem with a slip chart is the lack of a standard for

drawing the slip line. Consider, for example, the situation where 4 weeks of a 6 week activity have been completed with 4 weeks predicted work left. Some people will draw the slip line at two thirds of the activity duration (thus ignoring slip), some will draw the line at half the duration (reflecting half the work done and half to do), whilst others will draw the line at one third of the duration (reflecting 4 weeks still to do). The chart can also cause confusion if the users mix actual time to perform an activity with elapsed time (e.g. there may be four weeks work left to perform on an activity, but availability of resources restricts the completion until 8 weeks hence. Where should the slip line be drawn? I have seen each of the above practices used on projects, but my own preference is to use the slip line to show elapsed time until the end of an activity because I use the chart to help forecast when the next activities will start.

My reason for raising these problems with a slip chart is to highlight that, although the slip chart gives some good visibility of progress, it is only showing part of the picture. Other techniques for monitoring progress are needed and some examples are given in the rest of this chapter.

Another problem for the project manager who uses slip charts is the question of how to treat activities which have not yet started. If some of the current activities are slipping then is it likely that future activities will also slip due to a systematic error in the estimating process? This question is better tackled using some of the alternative techniques to gain visibility of progress which are described below.

Balls on the Walls

Slip charts are quite effective at monitoring progress, but they can sometimes fail to instil some urgency in the staff, especially when a deadline is looming. An alternative way of presenting the information from your PERT and Gantt charts, with an emphasis on setting targets, is shown in figure 3.2. In this example, the activities are represented by the lines and the circles (balls) are used to show start and end dates. For each activity on this chart, each ball can contain three dates. The ball at the start of a line records the first start date planned, the start date in the first replan (if there is a replan) and the actual start date of a particular activity. If a start date is replanned several times only the first two are recorded in the ball. The ball at the end of a line records similar information for end dates.

If an activity starts on or before the first planned start date then it is coloured green, otherwise the top half of the ball is coloured red and a replanned date is added. If the activity starts on or before the second planned start date then the bottom half of the ball is coloured green. If neither of the dates is achieved then the ball is coloured red and the actual start date recorded when the activity starts. The balls at the end of an activity are filled in in a similar fashion.

When such a chart is put on the walls of the office where the work is done then it conveys with graphical clarity how well the team is keeping to its schedule. When a project is slipping, the growing number of red balls motivates the team to try and create some green balls by finishing some activities within the plan. Hence, although relatively simple, the "balls on the walls" is a good technique for motivating a team to achieve tight deadlines.

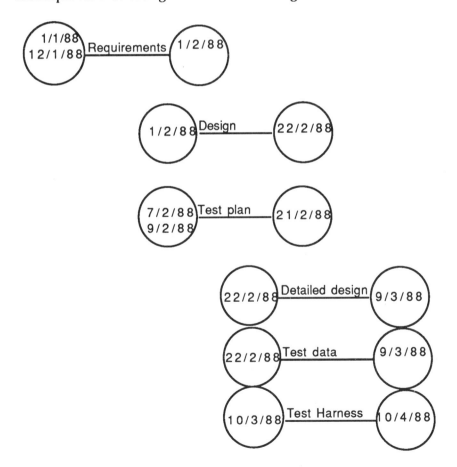

Figure 3.2: Balls on the walls

Accuracy of Estimating

We can never get away from the fact that a plan consists of many estimates so completion of a plan exactly on schedule is more correctly attributed to good luck than good judgment. In practice, those people who become known as good planners are usually those who include contingency and minimise the risks in a plan, rather than estimate accurately.

Planning is an activity that most people in a project get involved with because involvement in deciding the plan will increase motivation to achieve it. However, we can't all be expert planners and there is nothing like the feedback that experience provides to improve one's planning ability. Figure 3.3 contains a graph which shows, for each of those activities which have been completed on a project, their actual cost compared to their planned cost. This graph will show if estimates are consistently high or low, or if estimates are consistently inaccurate.

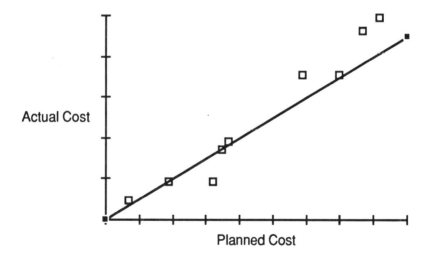

Figure 3.3: Correlation of actual costs with planned

An ideal graph is one which shows that estimates are randomly scattered to either side of the line where actual cost equals planned cost. Apart from giving visibility of the accuracy of estimating, this graph can help the manager identify other problems on a project. For example, if the project is slipping and the estimates are consistent with actual costs then staff might be performing activities outside the project. Unplanned activities on the project will show up as extra costs elsewhere in the project, but unplanned activities outside the project (e.g. writing proposals) can be hard to spot without this mechanism.

My experience with managers who see this graph for the first time is that they say "Oh, I knew that we normally ran over budget." However, when pressed further, they could not define by how much they expected to overrun. Is it 10%, 50% or even 200%? By monitoring results using this graph, I have found that managers are quickly able to quantify typical overrun for activities. By showing the results to the project team, this also provides a mechanism to motivate the team towards achieving and coming under estimates.

Resource Utilisation in a Period

Does a manager know exactly what the project team has been doing in each period? Progress reports (written or verbal) plus a knowledge of the key activities in hand will give an indication, but are they accurate? Is there a trend towards, say, increasing rework which hasn't been reported and may not be as planned?

The graph shown in figure 3.4 is a simple mechanism to inform the project manager what the project resources have been doing. It shows, for each period in the project to date, what type of activities the resources have been assigned to (this information can be obtained from timesheets). The Work in Progress (WIP) can be broken down into more detail (e.g. design, testing, etc.), if required, for greater visibility.

The graph of weekly costs shows the project manager the total amount of work done each week and the various categories of work being performed. This graph can help to highlight growing activities in non-project work (assuming these are charged to non-project accounts), increasing rework, etc.

In each period of the project some activities will be completed. These activities will have a known cost at completion which can be compared with the planned cost in order to calculate *achievement*:

Achievement = ((sum of planned cost of completed activities)/
               (sum of actual cost of completed activities))
             x 100%
for those activities completed in a period in the project.

Thus, achievement is high if the work has been completed quicker than expected. Achievement can be monitored in each period (see figure 3.4), but managers will have to use their own judgment to decide whether, say, low achievement is due to bad planning or poor work by the team involved. There may also be other factors involved (e.g. availability of hardware) which affect achievement so the manager must have wide visibility in other areas of the project in order to determine the root cause of low achievement.

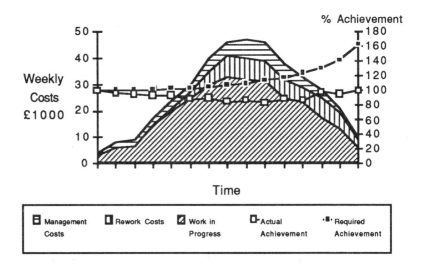

Figure 3.4: Weekly costs and achievement

Notes 3.4: The areas for each category show the total work done in each category. Work in progress is, in this example, all work except rework and management. Other categories can, of course, be used.

It can also be useful to record on this graph the achievement required for the rest of the project in order to complete the project on schedule. If there is a wide discrepancy between current and required achievement, replanning will need to occur. The example shown in figure 3.4 shows a typical scenario where low achievement over several months leads to an increase in the achievement required to complete the project on schedule. Although actual achievement has been rising in recent months, it has never met that necessary to complete the project on schedule. A new plan with re-estimated activities is required.

Some managers may wish to make a more detailed analysis of achievement by reviewing every active activity and estimating its current cost to completion. Although based on a larger sample of current data (rather than using data from completed activities), the results are much more costly to obtain and estimating is still involved. Hence, it is questionable whether the extra effort is worthwhile. If the manager has planned activities of short duration (say, two weeks) then the measure of achievement is fairly current anyway.

An ideal graph of actual achievement will show the project meeting 100% achievement every week (or whichever period this measure is monitored over). However, it is very hard to motivate staff to achieve 100% and a project manager often finds the team settles down to a "norm" between 80% and 95%. (This is another factor to consider when estimating!) If this continues for long then the required achievement will slowly increase if the project is to finish on schedule.

Resource Utilisation - Cumulative

The planning process will, hopefully, confirm that the project will be completed on schedule and within budget. The progress of the project can be monitored by simply accumulating the costs and monitoring the spend against the plan (see figure 3.5).

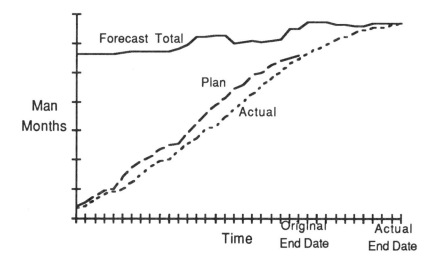

Figure 3.5: Planned and actual progress

As the project progresses, the project manager will have more information to improve the forecast of the cost at completion. I recommend that the predictions of total cost be recorded on this graph to help the manager learn how much these can vary during the project. This information, together with the trend of costs to date, can be used to re-forecast the end date.

Accurate re-forecasting of the end date is important to the project manager as it will indicate just how far behind or ahead of schedule the project is. If the project is behind schedule, it shows how large a change in the project operations is required to bring the project back on schedule. Alternative techniques for forecasting the end date will be discussed in this and the later chapters.

A measure of the actual costs is not necessarily a good measure of the progress because the work may not have achieved as much as was planned, i.e. after several months of work, the project may have cost exactly what was planned, but no real progress might have been made (unfortunately, this situation occurs far too often). One simple measure of the real progress on the project can be obtained by using an *earned value* calculation. The earned value at a particular point in time can be defined as:

Earned value = sum of planned costs
                        for all activities completed to date

Thus, if progress is on schedule, the earned value should be just less than the planned cost to date (the difference being the work in progress). Of course, if the current activities are slipping, the earned value will not be rising as fast as planned. In order to be able to monitor a reasonable level of progress in each period of the project, activity durations should be kept short. I prefer activity durations to be about 5 to 10 elapsed days.

The graph shown in figure 3.6 is one of the most effective that a project manager can use to monitor progress on a project. It is also especially good in helping the project manager to re-estimate the end date and final cost of the project. However, it only shows the project as a whole and a manager will gain better visibility of what the project is doing if the information is shown in greater detail. This can be achieved by monitoring the costs of resources in various categories. Figure 3.7 shows a graph of accumulated costs during the project in categories, together with predicted totals through to the end of the project.

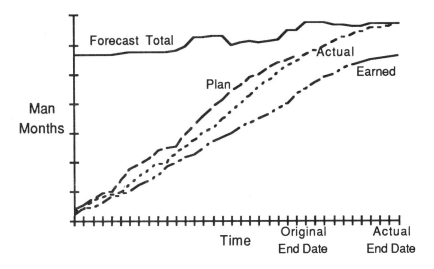

Figure 3.6: Planned, actual and earned progress

Notes 3.6: At the end of the project the earned value will equal the value of the costs in the original plan.

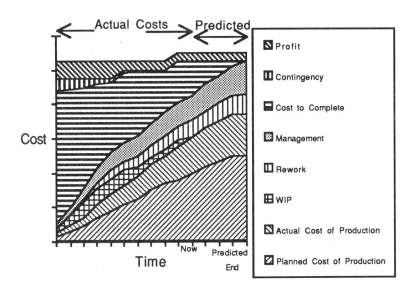

Figure 3.7: Cumulative costs

Some explanation of the graph in figure 3.7 is necessary. For each monitoring period in the project before time "now", the following are recorded:

(1)   *Planned cost of production* is the cumulative planned cost of activities involved in production (i.e. not management, rework, etc.) that have been completed.

(2)   *Actual cost of production* is the cumulative actual cost of activities involved in production that have been completed.

(3)   *Work in progress* (WIP) is the cost of production activities (design, coding, etc.) that are not complete.

(4)   *Rework* is the cumulative cost to date of activities which have been reworking earlier work (although this is rarely monitored directly on a project, its size does warrant the project manager having visibility of it).

(5)   *Management* is the cumulative cost of those activities on the project not falling into the above categories, e.g. project management, QA, planning. It does not usually include those activities which are supported as part of the company overhead e.g. recruitment.

(6)   *Contingency* is that part of the budget which has been put aside for use on unanticipated activities. It is used up as new activities are created or actual costs are greater than planned.

(7)   *Cost to complete* is the budget for the remaining activities.

(8)   *Profit* is the funds left over within the budget after all costs have been accounted for. It may be the difference between the costs and the price in a fixed price contract, or some measure of the cost benefit to a company which has funded the project under its own resources. In either case, if this becomes negative the manager should give serious consideration to halting the project.

These categories are presented as examples only. It is up to the project manager to determine which categories of work will provide the manager with most information during the project. Remember, do not have too many categories because this will only overload the graphs and the people that read them.

The example graph shows some major replans have occurred during the project due to the need to perform additional work (note the increase in the "cost to complete"). One of these replans was authorised by the customer to increase the price for the work. The predicted costs from "time now" are an effective way of predicting the final costs and end date for the project.

Although this graph is not easy to understand at first sight, it is soon apparent what it is showing and can be very informative during a project. For example, it shows:

- how quickly the contingency is used up (in the example shown it was used up before the project was half completed);

- the proportion of "overheads" (management, rework, etc.) used to achieve the planned production of the product (about 25% in this example);

- the trends to completion which indicate a predicted end date of the project, for comparison with the scheduled end date;

- sudden changes in the gradients of the lines at "time now". This has not occurred in the example given, but this sometimes happens when a manager wants to portray to his management or customer that the project will still complete on schedule. Sudden changes like this should be viewed with suspicion. Does the manager really believe that they are achievable?

Project managers can use this graph to evaluate the effect of certain types of changes on the project. For example, if rework levels are unexpectedly high, then the manager may choose to increase QA costs and monitor the impact on the graph.

Evolution of Budgeted Costs and End Date

At the start of the project, the planning process will indicate what date the project is expected to finish on and what the final cost of the project is expected to be. As the project progresses, the view of the end date and final cost will change as more becomes known about the product. In an ideal world, some activities would be done more quickly and some less quickly, so that the final costs and end date should not alter too much. However, experience has shown that some projects are grossly underestimated and they move into a situation of spiralling costs. This situation would be made more visible from an earlier date if the all the predictions for final costs and end dates were recorded during the life of the project.

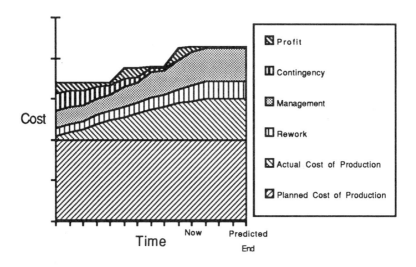

Figure 3.8: Historical view of predicted final costs

Notes 3.8: If a project had been proceeding on schedule then all lines would be horizontal. If one or more of the lines shows continuous growth over a long period then urgent action is needed.

The graph shown in figure 3.8 shows a record of the predicted final costs, broken down into several categories. It shows that the actual costs of production have risen during the project by about 40% over that planned. Together with increases in other costs, the result is that the contingency and the profit have been used up. Although the graph shows that from now onwards the predictions of the final cost are not expected to change, the history of this project suggests this might be optimistic.

The graph showing the historical record of predicted days to the end of the project (figure 3.9) will have a 45 degree slope if the predictions are accurate. Any prolonged lessening of this slope deserves investigation.

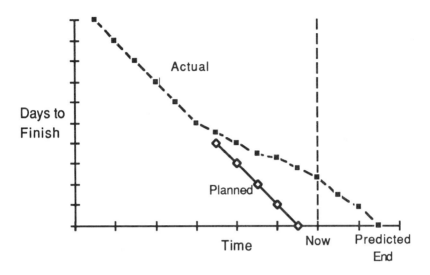

Figure 3.9: Historical view of predicted end date

Utilisation of hardware resources

Another view of progress can be obtained by monitoring the utilisation of hardware resources. The major hardware resource to consider in the development of software is that of the computer used to support development activities. As a means of measuring progress either the time spent compiling software, the number of compilations or alternatively the number of clean compilations can be monitored (see figure 3.10).

The monitoring of the compilation rate is inexpensive and provides an early indicator of the CPU power required in the future or of problems at the coding level. Once the compilation rate starts dropping steeply then the project manager knows the coding phase of the project is coming to an end, but failure of it to drop when expected requires management investigation.

The project team are always wary of the project manager monitoring their work, especially when it involves monitoring compilations. The project manager must make it clear that individuals are not being monitored, otherwise they may take action to make the graph "look good" (this topic is discussed in more detail in Chapter 8 "Implementing Visibility").

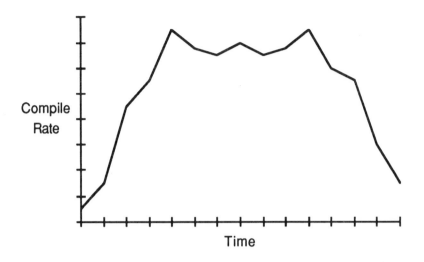

Figure 3.10: Compilation rate

PROGRESS VISIBILITY BY MONITORING THE CREATION OF COMPONENTS

As an alternative to monitoring costs on a project, the creation of a document, a module of source code, a test specification, components from structure diagrams, files of test data, lines of code or other identifiable components (sometimes referred to as products, not to be confused with the whole product) can be monitored to indicate progress. This type of monitoring should not be performed instead of cost monitoring, but rather to provide a new, independent view of progress. Production activities should not be recorded as complete until the components they have created have successfully completed a review or test and have been accepted by the quality control organisation. Any subsequent review or test should be treated as rework rather than production and is considered in later sections of the book.

Production in a period

The creation of components can be monitored in each period (e.g. weekly or monthly) and accumulated with time. The manager should be able to predict the production rate of each type of component so the actual rate will indicate if progress is on schedule (see figure 3.11).

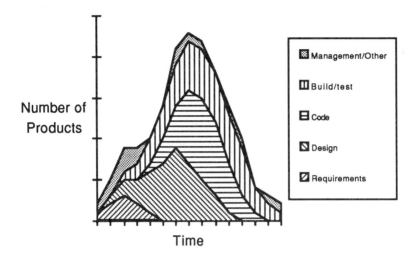

Figure 3.11: Weekly production of products

*Notes 3.11: Each area in the graph shows the total number of products created in a
certain category. Comparison between areas is not appropriate because the size and
complexity of products can vary dramatically between categories. What is most
important to the project manager is that the products are produced at a reasonable
rate. My own experience is that production of authorised documents can be zero for
several weeks until management issues orders for reviews to occur. This graph will
help the manager monitor production and ensure that peaks and troughs rarely
occur.*

The status of a component can pass through several stages so, if
these are monitored, the manager can obtain greater insight into
progress. For example, components can be:

- *In production.* It is useful to know that work has started.

- *Tested/reviewed at least once.* It is a milestone for a component to be
  able to be reviewed or tested, although it can still be a long time
  before it successfully passes a review or test.

- *Successfully reviewed/tested.*

- *Awaiting rework.* Following a successful review a fault in a
  component may be identified, necessitating rework. The cost of
  such nugatory work should be carefully monitored.

- *Undergoing rework.*

- *Stable.* Components in this state are separated from those that have not undergone rework so that the impact of rework can be assessed.

Sometimes, in their eagerness to appear to be achieving high production rates, some staff will "cut corners" in order to produce a component quickly. It is important that the QA staff try to ensure a consistent standard is achieved during reviews and tests in order that production figures are not distorted, otherwise repercussions may be felt later in the project.

Cumulative counts of production

Graphs showing the accumulated number of products in a particular category can also be produced. The values in these graphs can be weighted if this gives a more accurate representation of progress. For example, a graph of modules produced might be improved if each module was weighted by the number of lines of code it contained (see figure 3.12).

During design, progress could be monitored by counting the number of design components created in a structured design method rather than count simply the number of design documents. A count of the total number of design components can be used as an indicator of the potential costs in the rest of the project, but transformation parameters must be derived from experience on several projects before they become usable.

Another form of the graph shown in figure 3.12 can be used to show progress by showing the number of modules of code at each status. Many project managers currently ask their staff to fill in reports showing the status (designed, coded, tested) of modules each week, but this is laborious to complete and the project manager has to go through lots of paperwork before a real picture of the project's progress can be formed. The same information can be presented as a single graph showing total modules produced and the proportion in each category. Since this graph can be produced by the QA department based on their records of modules which have passed reviews and tests, the workload on the development team is actually reduced.

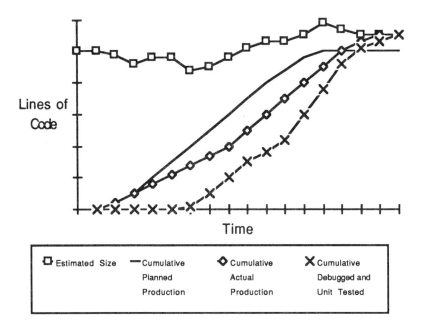

Figure 3.12: Programming plans/progress

Notes 3.12: This graph shows the planned rate of production in lines of source code towards the estimated total number of lines that are to be produced. As the project progresses, the actual production of code can be compared against the planned production. The completion of the coding phase can be predicted using the actual rate of production and a recent prediction of the total size. Often the first use of a module of code is to take it through unit testing and it can be useful to record the progress of this work on the same graph for an indication of progress.

Figure 3.13 shows the number of test cases that have been planned, produced, executed once and executed successfully (i.e. completed) on a project. When the achievement is extrapolated and compared with the target number of tests to be created, this graph can be a very good indicator of the progress being achieved and the date at which this phase of the project might be completed.

A common problem on software projects is a slow completion of tests. This can be due to a variety of sources (poor quality code, insufficient computer resources or inadequate debugging facilities) so the manager needs to monitor this work closely and have good visibility of other project activities so that any problems can be effectively tackled.

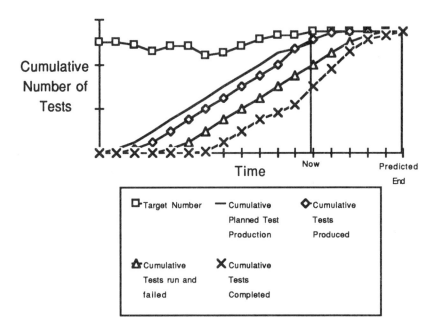

Figure 3.13: Test data plans/progress

Notes 3.13: The number of tests produced on a project can be measured in a variety of ways and a standard must, of course, be defined for the production to be accurately monitored. Normally, every line of test data is counted, or simply files of test data can be counted. A delay between first running a test and completing the test is normal because the first run of a test often finds a fault which needs to be traced and corrected before the test can be run to successful completion. However, if this delay is unduly large, the graph will provide the project manager with visibility of the problem. Note that, in the graph shown, the delay between running a test for the first time and running the test successfully appears to shorten towards the end of the project. This would not be a typical situation. Note also that this graph could be drawn independently for different subsystems or for different phases of the testing programme.

I have seen the graph shown in figure 3.13 used on several projects and, of all the graphs seen used on projects, this one has had the most impact. This is probably because testing is the least monitored of all project activities because testing is usually constrained by time limits rather than quality. When projects used this graph for the first time we normally found that achievement against the plans was very high or very low (typically the latter). This just showed that our initial estimates were abysmal. After using the graphs for several months we had learned a lot about the testing process and identified a number of bottlenecks which we had not even bothered looking for before.

Another way of looking at the progress of testing is shown in figure 3.14. In this graph the progress in testing modules towards an expected number is monitored alongside the hours of CPU time required to test the software. Apart from providing an alternative view of progress and an expected end date (of the module testing phase), the graph shows what CPU resources may be required in the future.

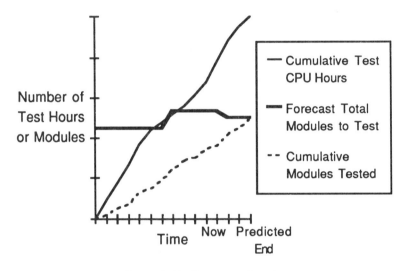

Figure 3.14: Progress of testing

Notes 3.14: It might also be appropriate to monitor the number of defects found during the testing process against this graph to investigate whether the testing is finding defects at a consistent rate.

If the testing team say they can increase their rate of testing modules then the graph shown in figure 3.14 will indicate what CPU resources will be needed to support the increased load. This will enable appropriate action to provide additional resources to be taken with plenty of time for their delivery.

The progress made during the testing phase of the project can also be monitored using some of the metrics presented in the next chapter on software quality.

PROCEDURES

Once the plans have been defined, it is important to monitor the project's progress against them. Every element of progress achieved gives us valuable guidance on how accurate our earlier estimates were and a chance to re-evaluate them. This does not mean that we have to replan immediately. The discrepancies we find between planned and actual achievement will normally be small and, in general, only after many weeks will they reach a level that requires replanning.

Although running the project to an old plan requires some form of control by the manager, it does provide the project team with a level of stability with targets they are committed to. A new plan could be produced each week in the light of progress, but this approach is costly and reduces staff motivation to achieve original deadlines.

Once a project has started work to a set of plans, all that needs to be done is for the following to be recorded:

- start and finish dates of each activity;

- resources used to complete each activity;

- products produced as a result of each activity.

Since activities are normally of several days or even weeks duration, this is only a small amount of information. This information can then be processed by hand or computer to produce all the graphs needed to provide visibility of progress.

BENEFITS PROVIDED BY PROGRESS MONITORING

Each of the graphs presented in this chapter gives the manager visibility of what has been achieved on the project so far and predictions of what progress can be expected in the future. These can be compared and used as a basis for reviewing future plans and deciding if action need be taken to correct any problems arising. In particular, the rate of progress achieved can be compared to that required in the future and, if there is a major discrepancy, the manager should review the justification that "it will be better tomorrow" (i.e. he should not assume that problems will solve themselves). The graphs will also help determine when replanning may be necessary.

4

PRODUCT QUALITY

INTRODUCTION

The quality of software is something we all appreciate, but find difficult to measure. However, there are a number of attributes of software which indicate its quality and it is these that we will use to give us visibility in this area. Just because they are indications does not mean that they should be ignored or treated lightly. The quality of the product will suffer if there are no controls over it when there is pressure on the project team to achieve targets in other areas (e.g. achieving the delivery date).

The basic definition of quality is "the product must meet the customer's needs." I have seen many projects fail because no-one ever stopped to ask the customer what their needs really were. Do they need a particular function, do they need microsecond response time, do they need 99.9% system availability? An important action for a project manager is to agree with the customer the acceptance criteria for the product. This must be done at the start of the project so that the criteria can be used to set metrics for use by the manager to control the project. If the acceptance criteria can not be measured then they are not useful. For example, "the user interface must be demonstrated to be user friendly" can not be measured, but "operators must be able to initiate any function within 30 seconds of sitting at a terminal" is measurable (so long as you have an agreed definition of what a function is).

Although the prime objective of most projects is to produce a single product, most activities in the project will each produce one or more component products e.g. a document, a module of source code, a test specification. The quality of the final product is dependent on the quality of each component and, like the links in a chain, the overall quality can be critically dependent on only one component.

Component products start being produced very early in the project so visibility of quality achieved can be obtained very quickly. Quality can be indicated by, for example:

(1)   team members, other than the author, reviewing a component.

(2)   analysis of a component using tools, when appropriate, which report on structure, complexity and adherence to "good" practice.

(3)   execution of the component, when possible.

(4)   the number of problems reported, changes authorised or the amount of rework.

A number of different mechanisms for monitoring the quality of the product are required because the traditional means of measuring product quality, counting the number of defects found during execution testing, can be a poor indicator. The number of paths through a software product is very large and, even if the data could be generated fast enough, most products would take hundreds of years of CPU time to test completely. Although theoretically possible, most paths will therefore not be exercised either during the tests or even through the lifetime of the product (see figure 4.1). A test team will make every effort to produce typical test data, but only time will tell how effective the testing has been.

Since quality is so hard to measure, the point at which testing stops and a product is released to a customer is difficult to determine. The graphs presented in this chapter give a project manager insight into the progress of testing and the likely quality of the product. These can be used as a more quantitative basis on which to decide "when has enough testing been done?" Experience over several projects will increase the confidence of the project manager in the quality metrics and levels used. I will return to this question later.

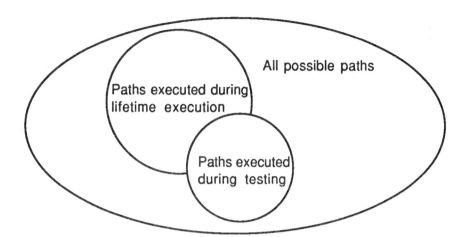

Figure 4.1: Paths through a software product

The number of techniques for measuring quality attributes of software are actually quite large. In order to provide some structure to this chapter, I have broken them down under the following headings:

- monitoring reviews and tests;

- problems and changes;

- software quality metrics;

- system and application quality.

MONITORING REVIEWS AND TESTS

Since software can not be thoroughly tested, the project manager must take action to measure the quality of the specifications to ensure they are not a major source of faults in the product. Monitoring the results of reviews and tests is not only a good indicator of the quality of the product, but it is also an indicator of progress (see Chapter 3).

When a software design specification is reviewed, it is possible that improvements to, for example, CPU power required, use of disk storage, interfaces, feasibility, might be identified. These improvements can be recorded as rework or as further actions to complete within the activity before it is considered complete. The topic of rework is discussed in a later section.

Reviews and Tests in a Period

Monitoring the number of reviews or tests in each period (see figure 4.2) of the project can often show the times when a team is under pressure, i.e. reviews and tests are not performed whilst some other activity is given priority.

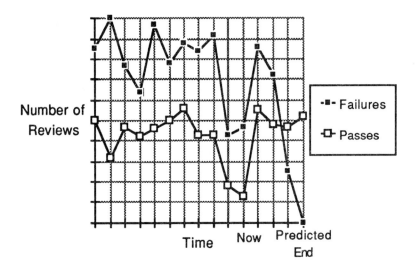

Figure 4.2: Reviews in each period

Notes 4.2: The gap between the "failure" and the "pass" lines will probably be large at an early stage in the project since basic human error will stop "right first time" occurring. Later on in the project, an increasing number of reviews will be second or subsequent reviews so they are more likely to pass. At the very end of the project we can expect few failures. Note also that the ratio of review passes to failures can vary from project to project. The example shown in figure 4.2 reflects some of my experience, but should not be taken as a guideline.

    If a project manager saw the graph shown in figure 4.2 for his project he should ask himself the questions "Is the recent drop in reviews due to expected circumstances (e.g. Christmas holidays) or does it signify cutting corners" and "How confident am I that the rate of reviews will return to its normal level in the next period?" Towards the end of a project, the rate of successful reviews can be derived from this graph and compared against the number of products remaining to be produced in order to calculate a forecast of the project end date.

Number of Reviews Before Success

It is also informative to monitor the average number of times a component fails a review or test before it passes (see figure 4.3). Too low a number might indicate poor reviews/tests, whilst too high a number might indicate a major problem in the product (possibly caused by an over complex design).

The graph in figure 4.3 also compares the results from the most recent period on the project with the results from the previous periods on the project. This has been done in case a drift towards weaker or stronger reviewing may be revealed.

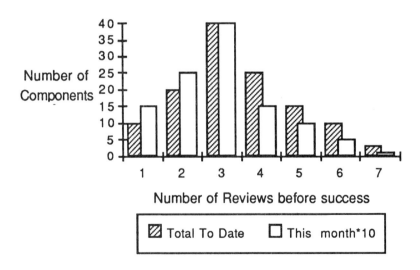

Figure 4.3: Number of reviews before success

Notes 4.3: This graph shows a comparison of the previous month's reviews against those during the earlier part of the project. To make the comparison easier, this month's figures are scaled by 10 (i.e. the number of previous months on the project). In this example, the average number of reviews to success is lower than in the earlier part of the project so the manager must investigate whether this is really due to improved quality, or the review procedures becoming more lax.

If a particular component requires a much higher number of reviews than normal then it deserves closer inspection by management. This may not be the most effective way for management to detect a problem, but this double check might be "better late than never."

I have found that providing project staff with visibility of the average number of times it takes to obtain a successful review helps them to expect, and to plan for, the need to rework after first review. It is surprising how many people expect to get it right first time! I hesitate to recommend an average number of reviews because the value depends on many project factors. As with most metrics, the manager must monitor the results on the project and satisfy himself that the results are reasonable given the project environment.

Defects found in products

A larger than average number of defects found in a component during reviews or tests might indicate further problems can be expected in that component. Alternatively, finding few defects might indicate that it has been poorly tested. In either case, management should investigate the product to see if a problem exists. Figure 4.4 shows an example of this form of analysis.

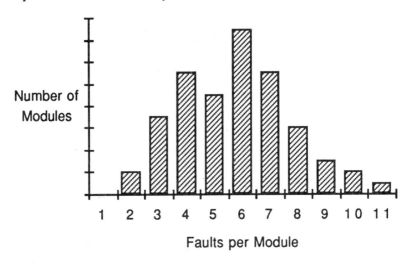

Figure 4.4: Defects found in modules

Notes 4.4: It is often appropriate to "weight" the results according to some measure of the size of a product (also see figure 4.24). This will overcome the problem that larger modules tend to have more defects.

Having found defects during reviews and tests, they can be categorised in order that the frequency of certain types of defects can be identified(see figure 4.5). Once it becomes clear which of the broad categories is responsible for most of the defects, the manager can take action to correct the problem or obtain greater visibility by breaking that category down into sub-categories. Initially, the categories of defects should be few and fairly broad since the staff will find it cumbersome to decide which of, say, 20 categories a defect should be associated.

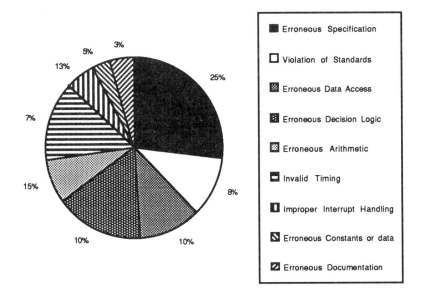

Figure 4.5: Defect frequencies

Notes 4.5: The figure shows 10 categories of defect in this example. Whereas the larger the number of categories that are monitored the greater will be the visibility provided, the large number of choices can cause confusion and annoyance to a test team who may have to fill in many forms. Often one defect may overlap categories so analysis of this graph requires care.

It is recommended that only 4 or 5 categories of defect are initially monitored and, at a later date, the largest source of defects can be broken into sub-categories so that detailed analysis can be made. The categories shown in figure 4.5 are appropriate for defects found in software code. When defects are to be put into categories which last for the whole project, more general themes are required. A possible set of categories, and some subsets, is shown in table 4.1.

When I have discussed the use of this analysis with project managers, I have often found them reluctant to monitor the project at this level of detail. My response to them has been "if you don't monitor these statistics how can you improve the quality of software development?" You must understand what problems are occurring if you are to stop them happening.

Table 4.1: Categories of defect

Prime category	Second category	Area of work
Alternative (or additional) operations preferred	Performance/User interface/ Standards	Operational software/ User documentation/ Test environment
Additions required	Enhancement/Omission	Operational software/ User documentation/ Test environment
Alternative required	Implementation	Operational software/ User documentation/ Test environment
Interfaces inconsistent	Configuration management/ Timing/implementation	Operational software/ User documentation/ Test environment

Thoroughness of Verification and Validation

It is almost impossible to justify the quality of software without some measure of the thoroughness of the testing process. Testing should be a lifecycle process (i.e. specifications of requirements and design should be subject to some form of testing), but it is only when the software can be executed that thoroughness can really start to be measured.

One form of test coverage measure is obtained by monitoring the execution of software during tests (this may require special test tools) and calculating, for example:

(1) the percentage of the statements that have been executed.

(2)   the percentage of branches (e.g. true and false branches in an "If" statement) that have been executed.

(3)   the percentage of the procedures that have been called.

These and similar measures can be made using a tool which inserts automatically statements into appropriate places in a product's pre-compilation source code. When executed, these statements update a data file which is processed later to provide the metrics. Before testing starts, the manager should define which coverage metrics are to be monitored and set a target values that testing of each component should achieve.

The testing of a system usually proceeds through several phases. Different measures of thoroughness should be used at each phase to reflect the type of testing that is occurring. For example, when I have performed bottom up testing, I have measured branch coverage during the first phase of module testing when detailed coverage is required, and I have used procedure coverage to monitor system testing when interface testing is more important.

The tools used to monitor the testing not only provide some metrics of thoroughness, but can provide an analysis of the components of the software that have been executed (see figure 4.6). These reports tell the programmers both what has been tested and, more importantly, what has not.

```
Procedure coverage report

Product name:   Printstring

Procedure name   Invocations

 Getinput           735
 Checkinput         735
 ProcessA            50
 ProcessB           496
 ProcessC             0
 ProcessD            32
 ProcessE           157
 Printoutput        735

Total number of procedures: 8
Percentage of procedures called: 87.5
```

Figure 4.6: Test coverage of a system

The visibility provided by these tools actually motivates testers to do more testing. It is then the manager's job to make sure they do not over test a component because it can be very costly to complete the last few percentage points (see below).

Monitoring the test coverage achieved for all components at a time in the project will also give the manager another view of progress (see figure 4.7). In the example shown, we can see that roughly one quarter of the modules have not started this phase of testing and almost one half have completed.

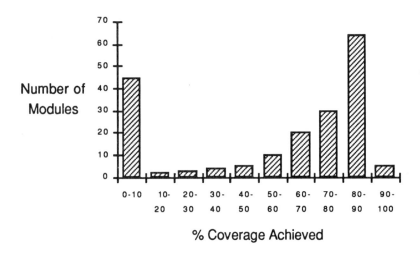

Figure 4.7: Test coverage achieved by modules

One's first assumption when setting a target test coverage level to be achieved on a project might be to aim for 100%. However, one must bear in mind that even 100% coverage according to these metrics does not mean perfect testing. As explained earlier, there will always be many paths through the code that have not been tested. The manager should set the team the objective of identifying the most critical 80% (say) of the code and then testing that. The test coverage monitor should primarily be used by the manager as a quality assurance aid to check that a minimum level of testing is being performed.

Another reason for not aiming for 100% of a test coverage measure is that it can sometimes be very expensive to achieve. Monitoring the coverage of tests has shown (see figure 4.8) that the first few tests can achieve high coverage quickly, but subsequent tests can have minimal impact. For testing to be cost effective, the manager must choose a number of compatible test methods and aim for appropriate levels of coverage with each.

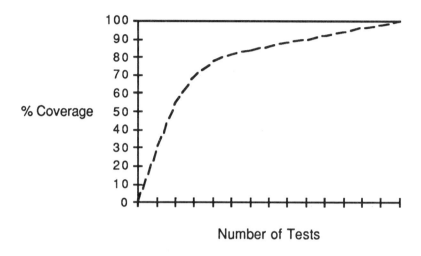

Figure 4.8: Coverage of tests

Note that I have found that software is only tested to about 50% coverage level by traditional testing. Once a tool is used to measure test coverage and show which areas of code have not been tested, the testers find that it is quite easy to raise the coverage level to 80%. Which coverage measures would I recommend? I have generally only used two on a project: branch coverage when testing modules and procedure coverage when system testing.

Yet another technique for monitoring the effectiveness of testing is provided by monitoring the number of defects found against the time during the system testing process. Time can be measured on a calender if the amount of testing per day is consistent, but it is often more accurate to monitor the hours of CPU time involved in the tests. With this information the graph shown in figure 4.9 can be drawn.

This graph can be very useful in determining when software can be released. There have been many research projects which have studied the rate at which defects are detected during testing and they have identified some algorithms which come close to matching the results. These can be used, together with data from the initial phases of

testing to predict when the failure rate will fall to an acceptable
level for delivery to be made.

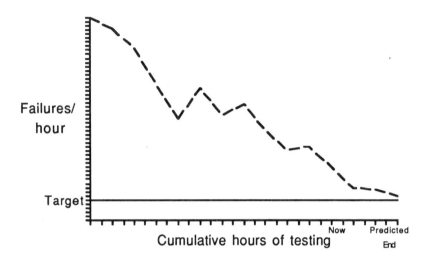

Figure 4.9: Failures per hour

*Notes 4.9: An alternative form of this graph can be produced by recording failures
per hour against hours of testing. A number of researchers have investigated the
theoretical shape of these graphs to see if they can predict when the target level will
be achieved. Although their efforts have been useful in some projects, the wide
range of factors affecting the shape of the curve make predictions difficult. However,
the graph is still a valid indicator of when software can be released and of the
quality of the testing (poor testing would lead to a rapid achievement of the target
level).*

Experience on previous projects will guide a manager in
determining an appropriate level at which to release the software for
the current project. A comparison of this date against other views of
the release date might indicate some discrepancy in the planning
process.

This explanation oversimplifies a difficult subject. Musa et al.
have written books (e.g. *Software Reliability: Measurement, Prediction,
Application*; 1987) on the topic and it is still the subject of much
research. However, although the theory behind predicting release
dates based on failure rates during testing is not perfect, the graph
does provide a powerful mechanism to monitor the progress in

removing defects.

If, after using the above alternatives for monitoring the thoroughness of testing, you are still not sure if you have done enough, there is another measure you can use. The process is called *mutation testing* and it requires you to take a working, tested system and to purposely install defects in it. The objective is then to take the mutated system and to re-run all your tests against it. If you only find half the defects you installed, then there is an *indication* that you have only half tested the system. An alternative use for this technique may be to use it as a tool to help indicate systematic problems with your test data i.e. are there certain types of defects the testers never considered?

I have never used this process, but it can be useful when you are testing ultra-high quality systems where safety is important. Generating realistic and random defects is not easy and it is surprising how much you can change the system without any visible effect.

PROBLEMS AND CHANGES

When a system component (e.g. a document, a source code file, a program) reaches a certain status in its development it normally comes under *configuration management* and *change control*. This requires that, from this point on, any change (i.e. rework) to the component should only occur following appropriate authorisation (based on the principle that we should monitor closely why there is a need to make changes to something that we have reviewed/tested and decided was good). If the project manager follows the principles described in Chapter 3 for monitoring progress, then the point at which change control should start is when a component is produced (i.e. it has passed its review or test) and an activity is completed. Change control nomenclature varies from project to project and can be quite complex. In this section I shall describe a relatively simple approach to change control in order to demonstrate the principles of visibility in this area.

Once a component is under change control it should not change, unless there is something wrong with it, i.e. there is a *problem* (e.g. a missing requirement, poor performance of the system). Problems are reported and then evaluated. Depending on the results of the evaluation the problem can be cleared without further action (e.g. when the report duplicates an existing report) or *changes* can be authorised to one or many components. An authorised change can be the result of a problem report having identified a *defect* in the components produced or as a result of the need to perform additional work (e.g. the customer has requested some additional functionality). The changes are deemed to be completed when new versions of the components are issued.

A large number of problems and changes can be recorded on a project, usually as the result of reviews and tests. Depending on the size of the project, this can result in the processing of many reports each day. Although the processing of problem and change reports can be seen as a chore, they can provide a manager with valuable insight on the work actually being performed on the project. For example:

- Why are many problems reported?   There may be poor relations with customers.

- Why is the cost of changes so high?   The reviews and tests in the early phases may not have been thorough enough, leading to expensive rework later.

- Why is there a backlog of problems?   There may be a large amount of unanticipated rework to do.

- Why is there a backlog of changes?   Too many people may be working with documents or code which is out of date.

- Why are there fewer changes than expected?   This could be due to poor reviews or testing.

Every organisation I know uses a different set of control forms to monitor problems and changes (some organisations now use computer based tools to monitor problems and changes, but the process and the information recorded is essentially the same). Often many different forms are used, but for the purposes of this book, I will present a simple procedure which requires only two forms. Examples of these forms are shown in figures 4.10 and 4.11. If your organisation does not have equivalent forms in use then these should provide a good basis for problem and change control.

PROBLEM REPORT

Reference Id

REQUEST

Originator:
Location:

Environment:

Date of Report:

Synopsis

Detected in (Item Name/Version Id)

Phase* Requirements/Design/Implementation/Build/Test/Operation(Delivered)/Other

Full Description of Problem

(Include additional sheets and hardcopy evidence where appropriate)

Detection Mechanism*: Inspiration/Review/Operation/Test
Severity of problem*: System failure/Loss of data/Incorrect results/
User recoverable/User documentation/Enhancement
Priority for action*: Urgent/Normal/Low

INVESTIGATION

Assigned to
Date

Date to be completed by:

Explanation of Problem

Category*: Alternative preferred/Additions required/Alternative required/
Interfaces inconsistent/Repeat/Not reproducible

Proposed Action* Take no action/Major Problem - Initiate Change by date

Request Rejected/Request cleared by Change Authorisations (list)*:

Authorised by: Date:

*(delete as appropriate)

Figure 4.10: Problem report form

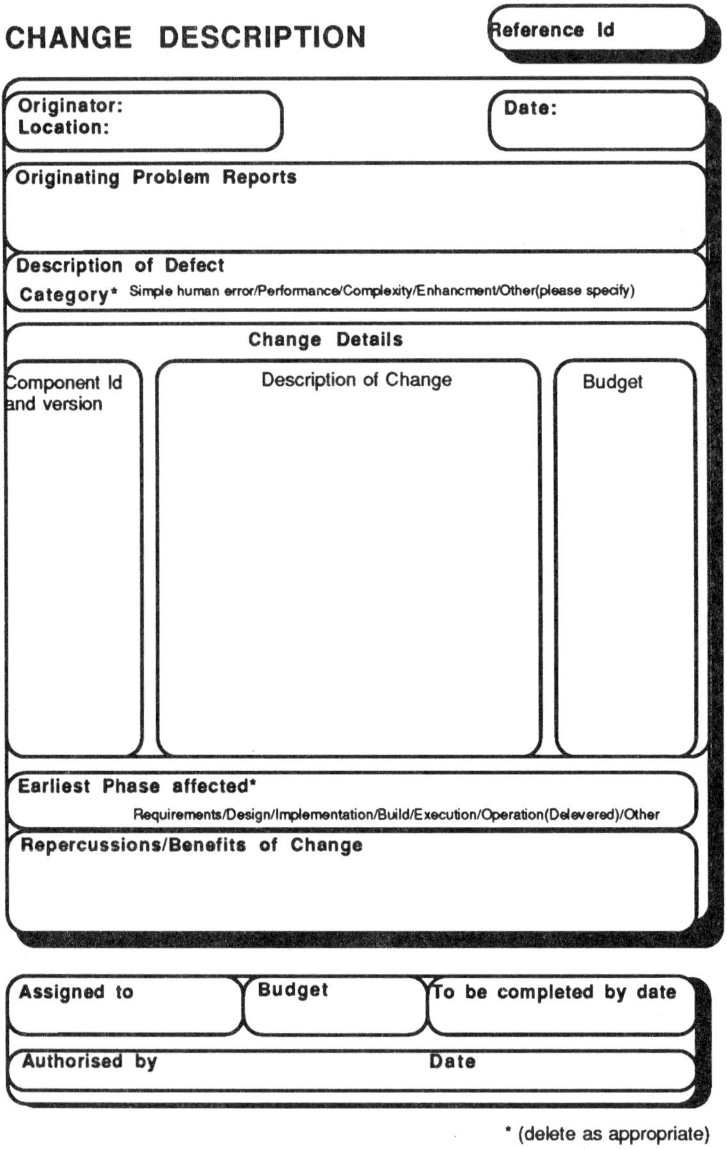

CHANGE DESCRIPTION   Reference Id

Originator:
Location: Date:

Originating Problem Reports

Description of Defect
Category* Simple human error/Performance/Complexity/Enhancment/Other(please specify)

Change Details

Component Id and version	Description of Change	Budget

Earliest Phase affected*
Requirements/Design/Implementation/Build/Execution/Operation(Delevered)/Other

Repercussions/Benefits of Change

Assigned to	Budget	To be completed by date

Authorised by		Date

* (delete as appropriate)

Figure 4.11: Change authorisation form

As the need for more detailed information and control becomes apparent then new layouts or more forms can be introduced. Some of the key words on the form are explained below:

- *Reference Id:*   A unique identifier for each form.

- *Environment:*   Specify the hardware and operating system environment (including version identification) in which the application software was running.

- *Phase:*   The phase of the product development in which the problem was detected. Customers would normally only detect problems in operational use of a system.

When does change control start? If products are brought under change control too early then many more changes will have to be monitored, whereas not monitoring changes until later in the project means only a few changes are monitored and the results are statistically useless. A useful guide that project managers can use is to require products to come under change control as soon as a second team member has to use them. It is also useful to tie this point into the planning/progress monitoring process by making it the conclusion of an activity. Project managers should be wary of comparing some statistics on change control across projects since the point at which change control starts may be different.

Problems and Changes in a Period

By monitoring the date at which each problem and change is raised and cleared, the manager can draw the graphs shown in figures 4.12 and 4.13. This can help the manager answer the following questions:

- Is the rate of receipt of problem reports and change authorisations as expected?

- Is there a trend which shows that the project will face difficulties in the future?

- Is there a backlog of uninvestigated problems which might lead to rework?

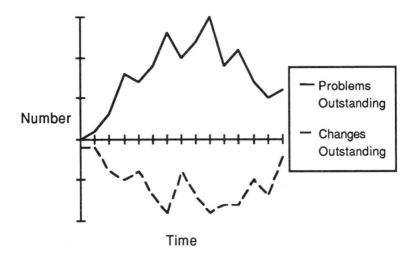

Figure 4.12: Outstanding problems and changes in each period

Notes 4.12: The time axis shows the zero line for the two graphs. This does not mean that there are negative changes outstanding. They have been plotted on a negative scale in order that the difference between outstanding problems and changes (i.e. the potential backlog of rework) can be highlighted. This is an important indicator to a project manager because it highlights the risk to the project of the team working with documents and software for which there might be changes to be implemented. It may be worthwhile for a project to present this graph alongside a graph showing progress through the testing work because the problems outstanding will normally rise when testing is being performed. It also may be appropriate to scale the graph by severity of problem rather than simply the number of problems in order to highlight the effects of serious problems.

The information shown in figure 4.12 permits a manager to monitor the backlog of problem reports and changes that have to be cleared, especially when both both are rising. I strongly recommend that a manager tries to keep the backlog of problem reports outstanding to a low level, because the sooner a problem is processed, the sooner the manager will have visibility of the impact of change required.

An alternative indicator of the amount of rework outstanding and the time it might take to clear it can be found in figure 4.13. This shows the budgeted cost of outstanding changes that have been authorised and the cost of changes that have been completed in each period of the project.

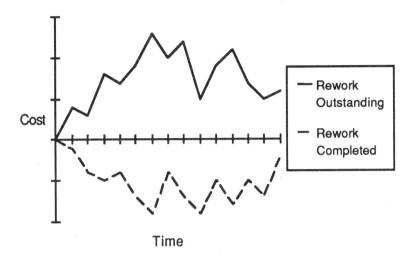

Figure 4.13: Rework outstanding and completed in each period

Notes 4.13: Once again a negative scale has been used to highlight the difference between the two lines. The values on this graph are scaled by cost, rather than number of changes, because this gives a more accurate presentation of the rework to be performed.

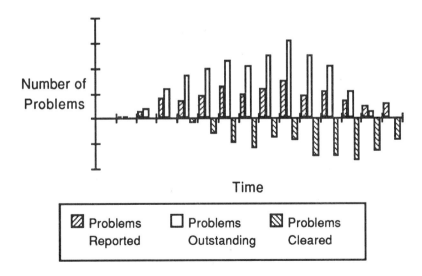

Figure 4.14: Progress of problems in each period

The information shown in figure 4.14 concentrates on the processing of problem reports. Unexpected high or low levels of problems being reported may indicate the manager should investigate an underlying problem. Alternatively, if the problems outstanding are growing then the configuration management staff may be overloaded. This situation increases risk for the manager because the reports might require a lot of rework that has not been planned/anticipated.

In figure 4.14, the problems outstanding are drawn on a negative scale to separate them from the problems reported and cleared, thus reducing clutter on the chart. A similar chart could also be drawn to monitor the progress of changes in each period. An alternative view of the effectiveness of coping with problem reports is shown in figure 4.15.

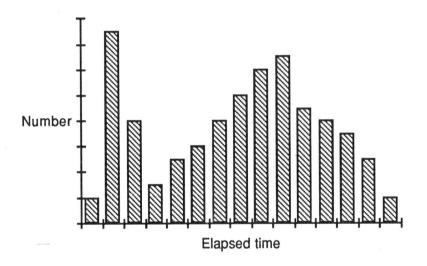

Figure 4.15: Response time to clear problem reports

Notes 4.15: Many problem reports might be easily cleared in a short time as they may require no investigation, hence the early peak in the graph. The second peak in the graph indicates the typical time that a problem report is processed in. This time should be monitored during the project since reducing it can improve staff effectiveness by reducing the time staff have to work with incorrect specifications.

This shows the time it takes for each problem report to be analysed and cleared. (Note that in the procedure I have described, a problem report is cleared when a change is authorised or the manager chooses to cancel it. The problem still exists in the product until the change is correctly implemented. If the average duration to clear a problem report is large, or is increasing in size, then the manager may need to take action.

One project where I used this graph showed an unexpectedly long response time for problem reports. A short analysis identified some obvious (with hindsight) bottlenecks in the process which could easily be corrected. In this case, the bottleneck was simply the internal mail system being used to circulate problem reports for comment. If we had not bothered looking we might not have noticed the problem.

Cumulative Problems and Changes

From experience, a manager can estimate the number of problems and changes expected on a project. As the project progresses, the forecasts can be updated as more knowledge is gained, providing the manager is convinced that a correction to the forecasts is reasonable. (It may be that the review and testing process is not being performed as planned.) The forecasts, together with the actual rates of generation of problem and change reports, will give the manager another view of the predicted end date for the project (see figure 4.16).

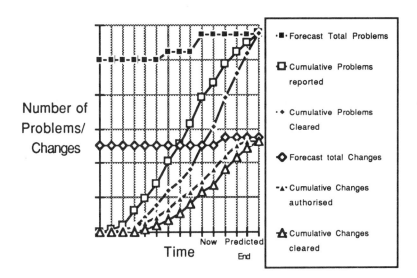

Figure 4.16: Cumulative problems and changes

Notes 4.16: This graph is rather "busy" since we are trying to monitor both problems and changes on the same graph. It is recommended that problem and change information is monitored on separate graphs. This would enable a planned rate of reporting problems and a planned rate of change authorisations to be shown on the graphs. Note that the difference between, for example, the problems reported line and the problems cleared line is an alternative way to present the problems outstanding (see figure 4.11).

The graph presented as an example in figure 4.16 shows a typical error a project manager can make. At the predicted end of the project, the forecast rate of problems being reported is still fairly high. This is not the situation I would like to see if I was wanting to release a high quality product. Of course, the rate at which problems are reported could be artificially lowered by reducing the amount of testing that is being performed. The project manager must be aware of this when monitoring the graph and making forecasts of when the product can be released. It is normally a good idea to present this graph alongside one showing the amount of testing being performed in order to give the manager a balanced view of the project status.

The problems can also be categorised according to the type of work affected during the lifecycle (see figure 4.17). This may indicate a particular problem area in the project, but this information often comes too late in the project for management to take effective action. This data is considered in more detail in a later chapter where the whole development process is analysed.

Problem reports can originate from many sources, hence it is possible a problem might be reported two or more times. This is recorded in the category "Repetition" because an unduly high number of repeats can indicate poor communication from the change control team back to the testers.

The pie chart shown in figure 4.17 can provide a useful snapshot of the problems, but it is also useful to monitor what types of changes are occurring at particular times during the project. This can be achieved by, for example, plotting a cumulative count of problems in each type against time (see figure 4.18).

The reporting of many changes of a particular type at a certain point in a project can indicate a problem in the development process (e.g. if problems are mainly found at the end of a project, they will make it difficult for a manager to achieve deadlines). Alternatively, the lack of certain types of defects may indicate that the testing process has a weakness.

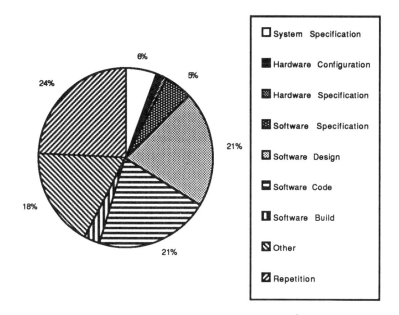

Figure 4.17: Count of problem reports by category

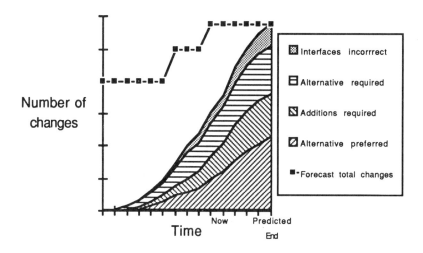

Figure 4.18: Report of changes against time by category

Notes 4.18: This graph could also be weighted by the cost of each change. I would normally expect the lines on this graph to have flattened out before the product is released.

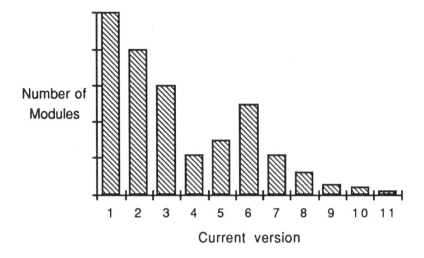

Figure 4.19: Number of products at a version number

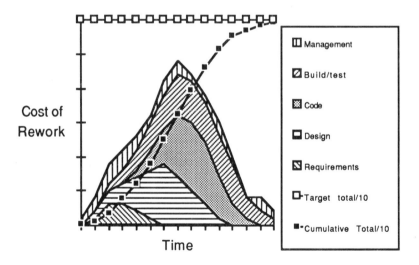

Figure 4.20: Rework costs

Notes 4.20: The cumulative amount of rework should be monitored against the original target level. This can be set either as a cost, or more simply as a number of changes to be implemented. By monitoring the types of rework as it is done during the project the manager can gain visibility of what the staff are doing at each moment.

When changes are implemented, the version number of the module being changed will normally be incremented. The use of the version number in modules permits a simple way to monitor how many changes a module typically goes through, and which modules are most impacted by changes (see figure 4.19). Those products that have high version numbers may warrant further investigation by the project manager.

Problems lead to changes, and changes mean the rework of earlier activities. At the start of a project the manager should set a target for how much rework is expected to occur during a project and then monitor how much occurs (see figure 4.20). A thorough analysis of the causes of rework can not normally be done until the end of the project. However, this knowledge of the level of the rework that is necessary, and the major causes of rework, will help managers make improved estimates and increase their control in future projects. This is discussed in more detail in Chapter 6.

I know that rework costs are rarely monitored on projects, usually because staff think that each change is "just a quick correction". On projects where I have closely monitored rework, the costs have been almost 30% of the total project costs. If these projects are typical, and I believe they are, then the amount of rework demands serious management attention during every project. Also, by monitoring rework and producing statistics like those shown in figure 4.20, a manager can defend requests to invest in tools which reduce the amount of human errors and the rework that results.

Effectiveness of clearing problems and changes

A manager often requires an answer to the question: "Is the project clearing problems faster than they are being identified?". The earlier sections in this chapter have presented some techniques for answering this question, but a simpler, clearer view may be useful. This can be achieved by producing a graph of the form shown in figure 4.21 (a similar graph could be drawn to monitor the effectiveness of clearing changes).

This example shows that, by monitoring the proportion of cumulative problems cleared against the cumulative problems reported, the manager can quickly see if the problems are under control. An upward slope towards 100% should be expected in the final stages of the project and a fairly flat slope in the middle of the project shows that problems are being cleared as new ones are being created. A downward slope, or a low plateau, indicates the manager may need to investigate the situation.

The graph shown in figure 4.21 is of most use to a project manager at the end of a project when a key objective is to "drive" the project towards resolving all problems before release.

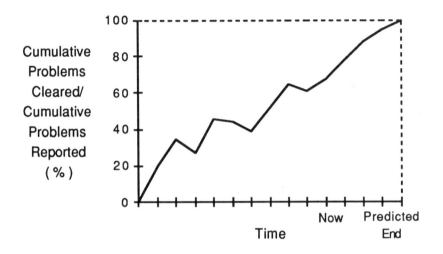

Figure 4.21: Effectiveness of clearing problems

SOFTWARE QUALITY METRICS

It would be nice to be able to measure quality and come up with a single number which quantified quality for each component of software. However, overall quality is related to a combination of many different characteristics, e.g. efficiency, integrity, reliability, usability, correctness, maintainability, verifiability, expandability, flexibility, inter-operability, portability, reusability and probably more - all of which can not be measured on an absolute scale. This difficulty has led many researchers into developing measures of the complexity of software code in the hope that they could be used to indicate the quality of the code and the likely number of defects it will contain (i.e. the more complex the code the more likely the code will be hard to maintain, unreliable, defect prone, etc.).

Some of the early work in this area, and certainly the most quoted, was performed by Halstead and McCabe. McCabe's measures are based on classical graph theory and they give an indication of the structural complexity of the software. For a component of software, he calculates its complexity using the following equation:

$$V(G) = e - n + 2p$$

where e = the number of edges, n = the number of vertices, p = the number of connected components and $V(G)$ is the cyclomatic number of classical graph theory which is used as a measure of complexity in this model. Various researchers have suggested that modules where $V(G)$ is over a value of 10 are too complex.

Halstead defined a number of measures of software structure and complexity, viz.

n_1 = the number of distinct operators (instruction types,

keywords, etc.)

n_2 = the number of distinct operands (variables and constants)

$n = n_1 + n_2$ = the vocabulary of the software

N_1 = the total number of operators

N_2 = the total number of operands

N = the length of the program

$V = N \log_2 (n)$ = the volume of the software, representing the

number of bits required to store the program
in memory

$D = (n_1/2) * N_2/n_2$ = the difficulty of the software

Whilst these measures have been applied to a number of projects, they have, in general, not been shown to be effective. Research is ongoing and there are many proposals for new, improved metrics. These all have their strengths and weaknesses and no single one could claim to be a true measure of quality. However, these metrics can be used to benefit by a development team because they can be used to identify "unusual" components.

During the project, the team can measure the value of a particular metric (e.g. complexity, as defined by McCabe) for each component (e.g. a module) of the product. Those components which have a high or low value of the metric (as highlighted in a graph of the form shown in figure 4.22) *may* deserve investigation, if only to be sure that they are different from the others for good reason.

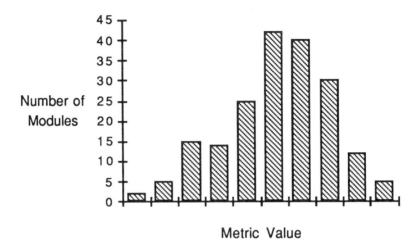

Figure 4.22: Number of modules against metric value

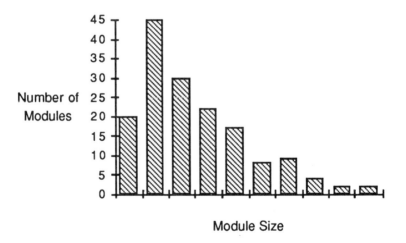

Figure 4.23: Size of modules

The size of a module as measured by lines of source code is probably the most commonly used metric in software development. It has been common practice in recent years to ask programmers to produce modules of less than 100 lines in order to force structure on the software and ensure modules do not become too complex. However, large modules can sometimes be appropriate for performance and other reasons. If the software librarian produces a graph as shown in figure 4.23 then the manager will gain visibility as to how closely the staff are following the project standards.

The number of defects found in a product is normally dependent on its size. If the defects found in products are recorded as a graph as shown in figure 4.24 then "outliers" on the graph might indicate whether some products have been poorly tested or are of such poor quality that they really need major rework.

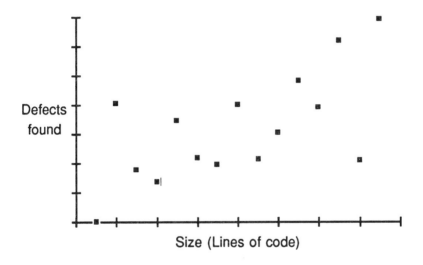

Figure 4.24: Defects found according to size of module

Notes 4.24: Outliers on a graph like this are those points which are furthest from the centre of a normal distribution e.g. a module of large size with a small number of defects. Note also that outliers do not necessarily indicate a problem. A large module with few defects might mean that it has been poorly tested or that it is of unusually high quality. Outliers need further investigation before action is taken.

SYSTEM AND APPLICATION QUALITY

There are a number of metrics associated with the process of building the system components to form the product (sometimes referred to as "the application" or the "system"). These are related in various forms with how one component interacts with another. It is not the purpose of this book to provide a comprehensive analysis of all these metrics (that could be the subject of a book in itself), but a couple of examples of these metrics (reuse and structure diagrams), and how they can be used to provide visibility, are presented below.

Also, once the system is built, there are a number of quality criteria associated with the application which must be measured and presented to a customer as part of acceptance testing. Examples of some that might be presented to a customer, with specific reference to reliability measures, are also presented.

It must be emphasised that the quality of the delivered product is dependent on the whole process of production (see Chapter 6). This means that, if poor quality measures are obtained at the end of a project, there is a risk that major rework of requirements and design, as well as the code, may be required. Hence, measurements of quality should never be delayed until the end of the project.

Reusability

Reuse of modules across projects and products should improve quality since the reused software should be thoroughly tested by previous use. A librarian could keep a count of how many times a module has been used, but I have yet to find a metric which defines how reusable a module could be.

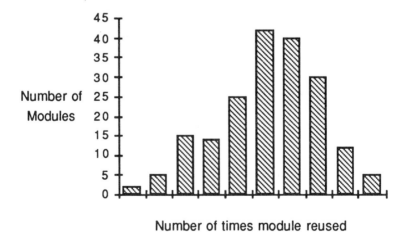

Figure 4.25: Frequency of module reuse

Within a product, modules perform functions on behalf of other modules. Hence, a module function can be reused by many other modules. Visibility of this form of reuse can be gained by creating the graph shown in figure 4.25. This will indicate to a manager the amount of reuse that is occurring within a product.Those modules which are most often reused deserve more thorough testing since a fault here will have major repercussions on the product. It might be more appropriate on some products to analyse the use of modules during the testing programme. By monitoring the number of times a module is called, those modules which are most frequently used can be identified.

The frequency of module reuse is not a true quality measure. It is presented here as a mechanism to indicate to project managers those modules on the project which are most important (i.e. most reused) and which should be of high quality.

Software Structure

Project staff will probably gain more insight into the complexity of the structure of software by seeing it rather than by trying to calculate a metric for it. The simple rule is that the more the program structure looks like a spider's web, the more likely it should be restructured.

Figure 4.26 gives an example of a software structure diagram. The diagram shown here is an appropriate diagramming technique for analysing the complexity of a product when only a few modules are involved. When a product involves several hundred modules other diagramming techniques must be investigated, or the system broken down into smaller units for analysis. The number of lines "fanning in or out" of a module (i.e. its inter-connectivity) indicate a module which the manager needs to be aware of. They are important to the system because they are "active" items and redesign may be appropriate if they form part of a critical path.

Similar diagramming techniques can be used to give a visual representation of the complexity of the code within a module (see above). These will help staff to understand which constructs lead to complex code and they also lead programmers into attempting to create "pretty" structures which are simple to understand and maintain. The use of structure charts does not mean that numeric metrics of complexity are unnecessary. They can still be used by a manager to provide an overview of all the modules as shown in figure 4.22.

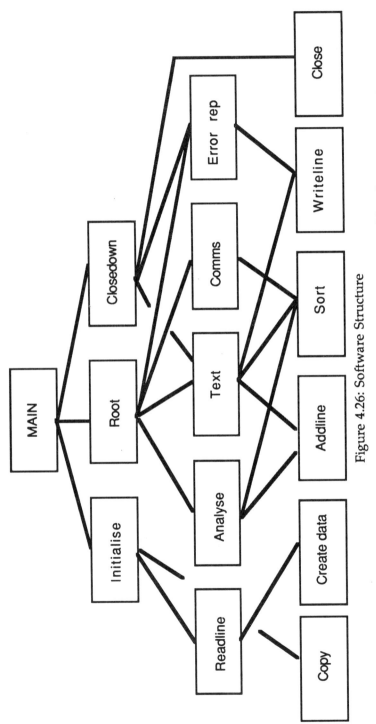

Figure 4.26: Software Structure

Notes 4.26: Each software component in the system is represented by a box. In this example, the connecting lines show the "uses" relationship.

System Metrics

System metrics (e.g. the utilisation of memory, CPU and I/O channels) can not be measured until the end of the project when the system has been integrated. However, the product will often go through many weeks of testing so utilisation of some system facilities can be monitored during this period to give early indications of their values when the system is complete (see figure 4.27).

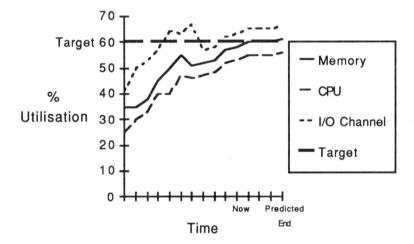

Figure 4.27: Resource utilisation in target processor

Notes 4.27: The target percentage resource utilisation can be different for each variable monitored. The utilisation levels will normally start from a low value during the testing because not all facilities are complete or fully utilised. The latter stages of testing are often orientated towards system tuning and this graph can help to show how effective this work is being.

A common use of a graph like this is to indicate which resources are approaching peak load and therefore impacting on system performance.

Reliability and Availability

A key question during any acceptance test is "will the delivered system be reliable?" The major problem for the project manager is that this is impossible to prove for a software system! The problem starts when trying to agree with your customer what software reliability means. People with a hardware background assume it is possible to measure software reliability in the same way as it is done for hardware. Unfortunately, hardware reliability is normally critically dependent on the aging of components, whereas software reliability is critically dependent on defects in requirements, design and code specifications. Therefore, the time when failures occur as a result of these defects depends on how the system is being used, rather than the rate or elapsed time of usage.

Trying to explain the difficulty of measuring software reliability to a customer who is facing frequent failures of their system is not going to release you from tackling the software reliability issue. You could try to blind the customer with science and spend weeks performing system tests and measuring failure rates (see figure 4.8). In a safety critical system, where there is little capability to test the software in a live situation, this approach is almost your only option. However, it is costly and doesn't necessarily reflect what the customer will be doing with the software.

Where safety isn't a critical issue, I would recommend that the project manager agrees with the customer for their staff to have a period for hands on use of the system prior to formal acceptance. In this situation, reliability can then be defined something like:

"If the customer does not find more than 2 critical faults and/or 5 serious faults and/or 10 simple faults in a period of 5 consecutive days of simulation testing by the customer then the system will be deemed to be reliable enough for delivery."

You will of course have to substitute your own maximum permitted number of defects and define clearly the categories of defects, but this is a practical way to agree acceptance where reliability is important.

But when does the project manager decide this acceptance test can take place? The problem has not gone away. I can not easily answer this question except to say that you have to rely on experience. If you measure a number of quality metrics you will be able to identify a point on the current project which you recognise is similar to the point on previous projects when acceptance testing started. If the customer requires a similar reliability for your current product and the last acceptance testing was successful, then you can predict that you will pass acceptance testing this time around too. I know this is very "hand waving" (especially in a book on metrics!), but this is the state of the art today.

I mentioned availability in the title of this section, not because I have a metric for it, but because it is again a metric which is important to your customer and is very often forgotten in acceptance testing. By availability, I mean both the duration that a system can be unavailable to the user and the proportion of time that the system is available for operational use, bearing in mind the time required for preventive maintenance, installing new releases, system failure, etc. If the product fails only once in a year the customer might think it is very reliable, but if it then takes three days to regenerate data files to recover the situation, then he won't be so happy. Hence, I would recommend you agree with your customer the availability level required and set metrics for certain features of the system, e.g. recovery time from certain situations.

WHEN SHOULD A PRODUCT BE RELEASED?

This is the most difficult question for a project manager to answer. The easy get out for a manager is to allow the customer or the senior management to bully him or her into releasing the product to meet their contractual or business needs. This abrogation of the manager's obligations inevitably leads to more costs and problems and the only professional response to this situation is to demonstrate to the client and/or management the potential repercussions of this action (I know this is easier said than done!).

The best way to handle this situation is to set some quality metrics at the start of the project and to monitor their status through the project. Extrapolation of the trends can indicate when a release date may be achievable and the potential quality of the product if the product is released early.

As has been shown, the quality of a software product can never be perfect so the project manager and the customer should both plan on a period of Beta testing of the product before "live" use. Real users often do the most surprising things and often identify defects in the first minutes of use, even after months of comprehensive system testing. I know of some project managers who use this scenario as an excuse for keeping their own testing to a minimum. It also gives the appearance of keeping development costs down. However, this procedure leads to many problems:

(1) The customer will test the system according to practical needs, but this testing is normally slow, random and far from comprehensive.

(2) If the customer finds many faults there will be loss of confidence in the system.

(3) Predicting completion of the Beta testing, based on quality metrics, is almost impossible.

(4) Costs for the development team in liaising with the Beta site testers to identify and subsequently correct defects will be larger than were they simply to test the product themselves.

In other words, a poor quality product, by almost any definition of quality, will result. The main objective for Beta site testing should therefore be to *prove* the system in a user's environment rather than to test the system. In other words, users should normally be looking for completeness of functionality, rather than correctness.

5

Support Visibility

We have looked at all the traditional elements of a project within a project manager's direct control, but there are a number of other factors which can affect the success of a project. In order to alter these factors to the benefit of the project, the manager usually has to persuade senior managers to take action, or even to spend their budgets!

Most managers will recognise this situation only too well from experience and lack of success. However, the solution can be quite simple - use the facts that visibility provides.

In this chapter we will consider 3 forms of support given to projects: computing facilities, organisation facilities (e.g. recruitment, accommodation, etc.) and sub-contracts to, say, engineering departments.

COMPUTING FACILITIES

A project is very dependent on the computing facilities provided to it, yet these are often not under the project manager's direct control. They are provided as a central resource to be shared with other projects and therefore priorities for their management can be quite different to those on one particular project. If a project manager complains that his project is suffering due to the lack of resources then it is probably too late to help the project because it can take weeks to obtain authorisation and delivery of additional facilities. Mechanisms are therefore needed to help a manager predict the support required and assist him in persuading the facilities management that more facilities are required. If the facilities are centrally managed then it is reasonable to ask the facilities manager to report to the project on the usage of the facilities, rather than the project have to collect and provide the information itself. Figure 5.1 shows one graph which can be used to monitor some aspects of the computing facilities (either for host development facilities or for "target" systems).

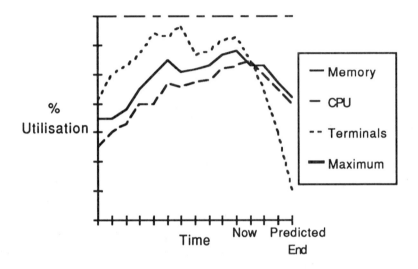

Figure 5.1: Computer facilities utilisation

Notes 5.1: This graph shows maximum daily utilisation of memory, CPU and VDU terminals. Depending on the type of usage, it may be more appropriate to monitor the average daily utilisation of the resources during normal work hours or over 24 hour periods.

Graphs can also be drawn to show utilisation of disk space, particular tools/computers, communication lines, e-mail facilities, telephones, test rigs or data entry clerks. Alternatively, the use of the facilities by particular applications (e.g. documentation, compilation, simulation, test, management) may need to be monitored in order to show whether the resources are being used to best effect.

In many cases project managers should not wait until there is 100% utilisation of particular resources before taking action because the project starts facing problems before this. For example, if the terminals have an average of 80% utilisation in a day then there will be many occasions at which a member of the project will want a terminal, only to find that there are none available at that time.

Also, although computer terminals may be available, a person may have to spend time looking for them. Hence, a project can start suffering from inefficiencies in working practice even when computing resources are not fully utilised.

ORGANISATION FACILITIES

A project must rely on its central organisation facilities for support in recruitment, accounts, quality assurance, supplies (e.g. stationary, computer paper), computer operators, secretarial support, training, accommodation (e.g. storage space or desk space) etc. As with computing, these facilities can be operating to different priorities from the project's, leading to insufficient support being provided.

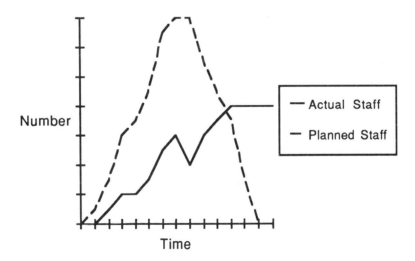

Figure 5.2: Staff Levels

One key area which affects a project is in recruitment. In order to "save costs", recruitment campaigns can be cut or the management may be reluctant to pay the salaries required to recruit staff. In these situations the graphs shown in figures 5.2 and 5.3 can help to persuade senior management that priorities must change. They may also be useful as part of reports to senior management and customers to show the cause of any slip in a project.

On some occasions a project may have the correct total numbers of staff, but an inappropriate mix of skills since it is easier to recruit low skilled rather than skilled staff. It is important to monitor the skills available (see figure 5.4) and compare them against the plans because this may be the only explanation for a slip occurring on a project.

Very often projects go awry because the planners assumed that staff can do 5 days of work in 5 days. This is rarely the case because staff have many calls upon their time apart from performing "real" work. Consider, for example:

* Sickness;
* Holidays;
* Training;
* Management meetings and preparing reports for them;
* Union meetings and preparing reports for them;
* Customer meetings and preparing reports for them;
* QA audits and inspections;
* Project coordination meetings and preparing reports for them;
* Preparing plans for future work and providing reports on progress to date;
* Preparing proposals for new projects;
* Providing support to other projects;
* Interviewing potential recruits;
* Appraising current staff, or being appraised;
* Birthday, Christmas or company parties.

With such a long list one sometimes wonders when the staff can ever get time to do some real work. These overheads are not constant and, if they are not monitored, then the project can end up supporting all sorts of other activities within its budget. For example, on one project I was working on, the project manager monitored the team's use of time over just a few weeks to find out why we were always slipping on our plans. It soon became evident that the team were doing many "project related" and company support activities that did not directly benefit the project's timescales or budgets. Since the project manager's bonus was based solely on completing the project within deadline and budget, it didn't take him long to correct this situation.

Figure 5.3: Staff turnover

Note 5.3: This example shows that recruitment (staff joining) lags far behind the plan (plan staff joining) and that there have been several unplanned leavers. Note that leavers can be planned, based on known staff movements and normal staff turnover rates. The end result on the project from which this graph is drawn is that their staff levels are way below plans which is a major factor in any slippage of the project milestones.

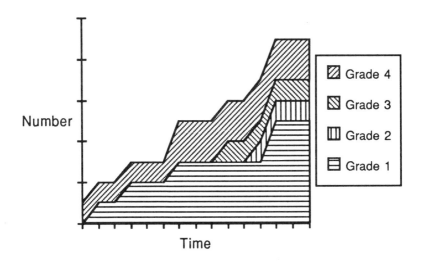

Figure 5.4: Skills available to a project

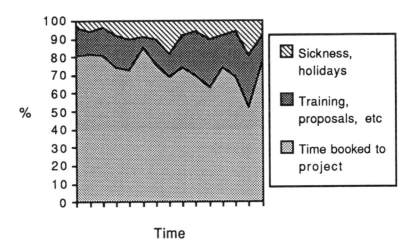

Figure 5.5: Resource utilisation

Notes 5.5: Time not spent doing direct project work can be most easily monitored by allowing staff to book such time to a "bucket" activity (i.e. an activity with no deliverables). This improves honesty in reporting. If such activities are not monitored then there is a tendency for them to grow.

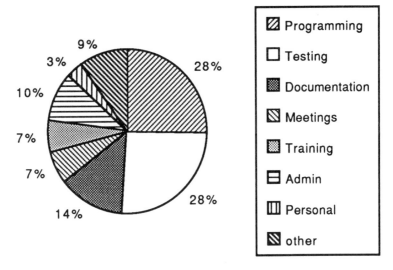

Figure 5.6: How programmers spend their time

The graph shown in figure 5.5 will help a manager monitor these overheads and it will also provide valuable feedback to the estimators and planners as to what levels of elapsed time they should allow for activities.

Another way to analyse what the staff are really doing on a project is shown in figure 5.6. It shows the proportion of time spent on different classes of work.

SUB-CONTRACTS

In many organisations the project manager will sub-contract parts of the work off to other sections of the organisation. Some items of work will form mini-projects and these can be monitored using the techniques described elsewhere in this book. However, some items of work will be of a small and repetitive nature so a different form of monitoring is appropriate. Consider, for example, the support provided by the word processing centre in turning around documents, or in an engineering section which provides printed circuit boards according to a design. For such items of work it can be worth while to monitor the response times (turnaround times) from issue of order to receipt of delivery (see figure 5.7).

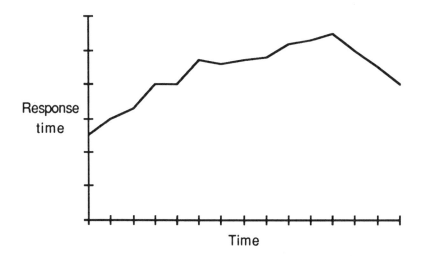

Figure 5.7: Response times from engineering department

6

PROCESS VISIBILITY

The process of developing software involves the project management procedures (e.g. organisation, configuration management), the methods used by the project team (e.g. requirements analysis, design techniques) and the tools used by the team. Visibility of the effects of the process will provide evidence of the effectiveness of a particular process or of a change to the process.

The earlier chapters of this book provide a manager with techniques which will give visibility of progress and product quality, as well as the impact of the support services. The progress and product quality are dependent on the process used for development, but other factors (e.g. the impact of support services, the skills and level of training of the staff employed) can have greater effect than the process. Hence, good visibility of these factors is needed before visibility of the process can be studied.

Some people will argue that software engineering is still an immature discipline and that it will be a long time before we can understand the process of software development. However, some of the effects of a process can be made visible by comparing the results of one project with that of another, by analysing and trying to understand some of the characteristics of a particular process, or simply by monitoring the utilisation of resources on the various project activities. For example, a project manager will be able to improve the process of software development if the answers to the following questions are known:

- How many defects have occurred, where did they occur and what was the cost of the resultant rework?

- How long has it taken to perform certain types of activities, what factors delayed their conclusion and is this typical on other projects?

Once the project manager has a better understanding of the development process, some of the actions that can be taken to improve the process include:

- Automate some of the activities, but which ones will give most cost benefit?

- Reduce rework, but where is it originating from today?

- Reuse components;

- Provide people with the right environment to facilitate productivity.

COMPARING THE RESULTS OF PROJECTS

Every project has different characteristics so it can be difficult to compare results between them. However, the monitoring of a number of variables, as described in the earlier chapters, can give greater visibility of the key characteristics of the projects and make comparisons feasible. A few examples of comparisons that could be made are:

- comparing the proportions of the total project costs on rework, QA, management, planned production, actual production costs, etc.;

- comparing the numbers of problem reports, change authorisations;

- comparing the amount of time spent in each development phase of the project;

- comparing the time spent on reviews, the defect rates found in modules, the types of defects found.

The comparisons should show up good and bad practices, thus enabling the process on future projects to be improved. If significant differences can't be explained then a manager should consider monitoring additional information on future projects to try to determine the source of improvement.

A major effect of changing the process will be to change the proportions of costs in the various phases of the development lifecycle. This can be monitored on graphs of the form shown in figures 6.1 and 6.2.

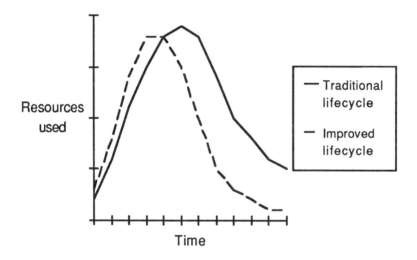

Figure 6.1: Lifecycle costs

The graph shown in figure 6.1 presents a theoretical objective, i.e. we would like to use an improved development lifecycle which results in lower overall cost. To measure the benefits of a new development lifecycle in practice is very difficult because there are many factors involved (e.g. the difficulty of the development and the people doing the work will vary from project to project). However, if we have determined certain weaknesses in our current development lifecycle then we can monitor the effects of our corrective action to see if our objectives are being achieved.

The graph shown in figure 6.2 shows the effect of requiring our development teams to concentrate more effort in ensuring the correctness and consistency of project specifications. The result is that a smaller proportion of their time is spent in the implementation phase. Of course, to see if our changes are having beneficial impact, we must also monitor the proportion of projects coming within budget and deadlines. If this is increasing year on year then our improvements are having real benefit.

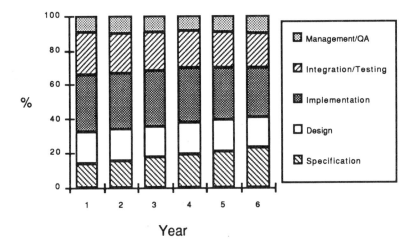

Figure 6.2: Proportion of costs in lifecycle phases

Note 6.2: If a company has many ongoing projects then it can monitor the costs of each phase of work in each year and compare them directly. If the company has some large projects which run over several years then the effects of these should be removed before this graph is drawn.

UNDERSTANDING THE PROCESS

In order to gain a deeper understanding of the process of software development we must identify where time or resources are being used, where they are being wasted (for example, in rework or poor utilisation of resources) and where work can be done more efficiently and effectively (e.g. by different grades of staff or by automatic/mechanical means).

Rework

Rework is caused by the resources (staff or their tools) making mistakes, or by the customer changing the requirements. The process can be improved if we can answer the following questions:

- What types of defects are occurring?

- Where are the defects occurring?

- Can the defects be detected earlier?

If we can answer these questions then we should be able to take action to reduce the frequency of defects. This should result in managers being able to produce graphs like those in figures 6.3 and 6.4.

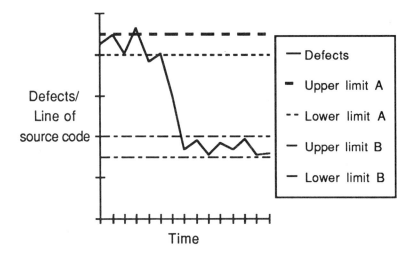

Figure 6.3: Statistical control chart

The graph presented in figure 6.3 shows the defect rate of projects at their date of release over a period of years. In the early years, the defect rate was expected to fall within the targets (A) shown; any project with a defect rate outside the range needs investigation. Too high a rate indicates normal quality levels are not being achieved and too low a rate may mean poor testing. If a source of defects is detected and removed then lower bounds (B) can be set as targets for controlling the quality of projects. In practice, major improvements in the defect rate are not made quickly and a slow improvement over several years is all that can be achieved, as shown in a more realistic graph presented in figure 6.4.

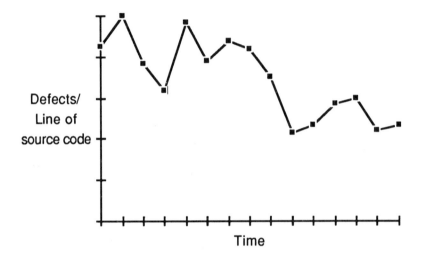

Figure 6.4: Defect density

Notes 6.4: Each point represents the defect density for a project at the time that it is released.

Figure 6.4 shows that over a period of years the defect rate of products on their first release to a customer should be falling if the process improvement actions are being effective. Such a graph is also good for providing customers with the confidence that this supplier is knowledgeable and that they can expect even better quality in the future.

The Cost of Change

Although removing the cause of defects is an ideal way of improving the process, it is not always applicable. However, the cost of rework following the detection of a defect can be high, so it is worth investigating what costs are involved and if they are higher in some areas than others (see figure 6.5).

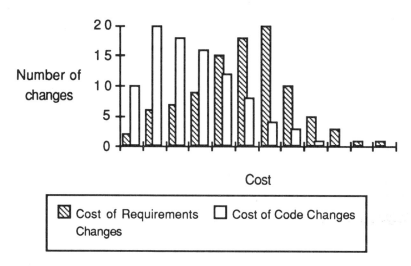

Figure 6.5: Cost of changes

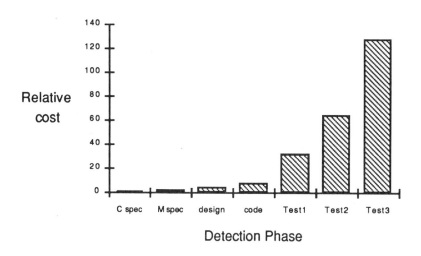

Figure 6.6: Cost to repair a defect in the customer specification

Notes 6.6: The C spec. and the M spec. are the customers's specification and the manufacturer's specification, respectively. The testing on this project was broken down into 3 phases: Test1, Test2 and Test3.

The cost of a change will vary according to the time when it is detected because the later it is detected the more rework that will be necessary. If the cost to repair a defect in, say, the customer's specification is monitored against the phase at which the defect is detected then a graph like that shown in figure 6.6 can be drawn. The very high costs shown for correcting defects that are not found until the end of a project are not untypical.

What was the cause of a change?

Monitoring the number of changes being authorised on the project can assist a manager, but long-term benefit can only be obtained if the causes of change can be identified. This can be done by analysing the changes and identifying *root changes* separate from *repercussion changes*. (A root change in, say, a design component might have repercussion changes in source code modules, test specifications, user documentation and system builds. However, it is the change to the design component which is most important to our analysis because, if the need for a change is detected late in the project then the cost of the overall change increases dramatically due to the greater number of repercussions. Note that in figures 6.5 and 6.6 the cost of a change included the cost of all the repercussion changes.)

If this information is collected during the whole of the development lifecycle, together with a record of how and when the need for a change was detected, the histograms shown in figures 6.7 to 6.10 can be created. These indicate, for each defect that results in a change, which phase of the development the defect was detected in and in which phase it was created (the root of the change). The number of repercussion changes are not counted in the results, but their cost is included in the cost of the root change.

Figures 6.7 and 6.8 show the number and costs of changes respectively, according to the phase of the project at which the need for a change was detected. These figures show that, although most changes were identified early in the project, the major cost in rework is due to those changes not identified until first level testing. The figures also can indicate which are the best techniques for detecting defects. In the example shown, it is clear that the first phase of testing has been the most effective phase for detecting defects, in terms of cost of resultant rework.

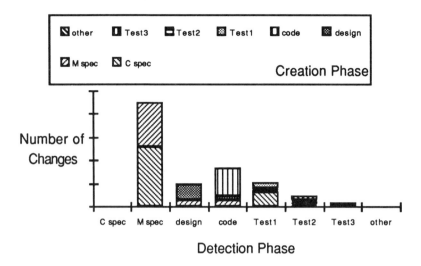

Figure 6.7: Number of changes according to phase of detection

Notes 6.7: The first indication from this graph is that the project team did well to identify the majority of changes early on in the development. However, the number of changes is not a good indicator of efficiency.

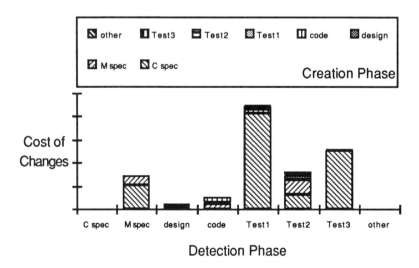

Figure 6.8: Cost of changes according to phase of detection

Notes 6.8: When figure 6.7 is redrawn to show the costs of the changes, it becomes clear that a large proportion of the cost of the rework is due to not detecting changes in the requirements until the testing phases of the project.

In figures 6.9 and 6.10 the histograms show the same information according to the root (creation phase) of the changes. When figure 6.9 is redrawn to emphasise the costs of the changes (see figure 6.10), it becomes obvious that the vast majority of the cost of the rework originated from the defects in the customer specification. Hence, if only a little more time had been spent checking this specification, rework costs would have been much reduced and a better quality product could have been delivered early. In this particular company, a project manager could easily justify increasing the costs of analysis of the customer specification on future projects in order to save costs in rework.

The results obtained from figures 6.7 to 6.10 can be used by a project manager to identify the key phases of any project which are causing rework. In fact, the graphs presented here were the results from a real project. The project manager monitored all changes closely because the software was for a safety critical application. Even though the application was critical, the customer rushed through the customer specification because "everyone knows how to implement this functionality, we've done it several times before and timescales are tight so let's rush on."

Initially, the project manager was pleased that a large number of defects in the customer specification and his own specification were highlighted in the early stages of the project. This seemed to indicate that the project would at least proceed from that point with a good quality specification. It was not until the end of the project that the project manager gained full visibility of the impact of changes on the project.

With this new information, the project manager was able to show that the poor requirements specification with which his customer forced the project to start, led to over $400,000 of rework during the project. The project manager had no problems when he tried to persuade the same customer to spend $200,000 on requirements analysis at the start of the next project. The knowledge he had gained also enabled him to persuade other project managers and their customers that quality of requirements specifications is critical.

If we applied this analysis to your project, do you know what result we would find? I usually receive the answer "Yes, the same result as shown here", but further investigation shows that the manager has done nothing to create this type of analysis to persuade their senior management or customers to change practices. Why are managers so disinterested in improving their work?

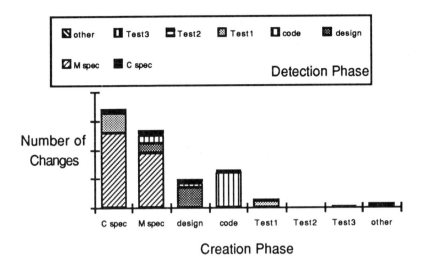

Figure 6.9: Number of changes according to the source of defect

Notes 6.9: This graph shows the same information as shown in figure 6.7, but the category information along the bottom of the graph now shows the phase at which defects were created. This indicates that the customer specification was the major source of defects.

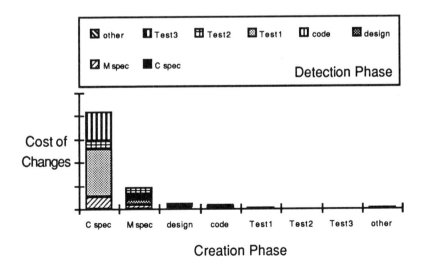

Figure 6.10: Cost of changes according to the source of defect

More details of specific types of defects are sometimes needed. In the chapter on product quality some graphs were presented showing the causes of defects in products. This information can be used to reduce their frequency, but there are some additional approaches to reducing the frequency of defects; consider for example the graph shown in figure 6.11.

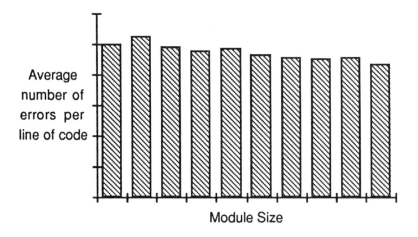

Figure 6.11: Defect rate according to the size of a module

This graph shows that larger modules of source code contain slightly, but significantly, fewer detected defects. Although this might be counter to the arguments that small modules are less defect prone because they are necessarily simple, such results have been found in practice. They have been explained by the fact that larger modules can be easier to implement because they have fewer interfacing problems. However, an alternative viewpoint is that such modules are hard to test so fewer defects will be detected. Whether these results are valid or not, such measurements do indicate ways in which the process of development can be analysed in order to identify areas for improvement.

MONITORING THE RESOURCE UTILISATION

Many activities in the development process can be monitored in order to determine whether they can be improved by reassignment of effort and skills or by automating manual tasks. Some examples of monitoring the work have been given in previous chapters, but another example is the monitoring of rework to find out how long it takes to fix a defect once it has been identified (see figure 6.12).

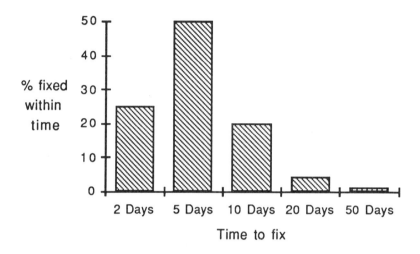

Figure 6.12: Defect fix times

Notes 6.12: This graph shows the elapsed days used to fix some defects. The longer a defect is outstanding, the greater the risk of problems for users of the product. It would also be useful to monitor the actual man-hours to fix defects since this is a real cost to the project.

There are a number of factors which affect the duration to fix defects, but often one will be dominant. Some examples of activities that could be monitored closely are:

- system rebuild duration and frequency of rebuilding;

- system test duration;

- time to evaluate and debug a problem report.

7

VISIBILITY OF MAINTENANCE

Once a project has been completed and the product has been delivered work rarely stops. The product may need to be enhanced to meet additional customer requirements, or faults may be found which were missed during the product development. Over the lifecycle of a product, from delivery to obsolescence, the maintenance costs may equal that of the original development.

A software product can be in use over many years during which time staff will change and knowledge will be lost. It is therefore very important that the manager of a maintenance programme has good visibility of the effectiveness of the work in order to keep standards high.

Note that the examples of metrics presented in this chapter are from a single product. If the data is to be compared against other products then a number of other factors (e.g. size of product, duration that product has been in the field) have to be taken into account before valid comparisons can be made.

TIME TO RESPOND TO A PROBLEM REPORT

During their use of a product, customers will identify what they think are problems with the product and they will raise problem reports.

The time it takes the maintenance team to respond to a problem report will be used by the customer as one indication of the quality of the support they receive. In order to keep this time visible and under control a manager can produce a graph like that shown in figure 7.1. (Note that the time to respond to a problem report is simply the time it takes to acknowledge the customer's report and confirm the action to be performed by the maintenance team. It is not the time it takes to correct the problem; this is discussed later).

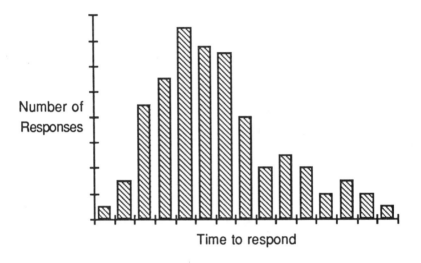

Figure 7.1: Time to respond to problem reports

Notes 7.1: The problem reports that take greatest time to process deserve further attention from a manager in order to attempt to reduce the likelihood of long response times in the future. The most likely response time should also be monitored in order to try and reduce that too. What are the main factors that delay a response?

I have found that it is only necessary to produce the graph shown in figure 7.1 occasionally because the profile of the graph does not change rapidly from one month to the next. However, metrics I do recommend to be monitored each month are:

(1) for the current problem reports, the average time they have remained open without, say, a patch or work around being sent to the customer;

(2)   for problems closed in the last month, the average response time and the time it takes to respond to 95% of the problems.

These metrics give a simple and effective guide each month to whether the situation is improving or not. They are extremely effective at setting targets for a team to improve the response to customers' requests.

TIME TO CORRECT PROBLEMS

Once a problem has been identified the customer will be waiting anxiously for the next release of a product. However, not all problems can be dealt with immediately or resolved before the next release. Visibility of the level of customer dissatisfaction can be gained by monitoring the duration that problems have been outstanding (see figure 7.2) and the number of problems outstanding at any time (see figure 7.3).

The duration that problems have been outstanding is often a critical metric for a maintenance team because there might be contractual commitments to resolve problems within a specified period. Even when its not a contractual commitment, a target can be set for a maintenance team to achieve. Rather than plot all the problems on one graph, I have usually broken the problems into categories (e.g. critical, major and minor problems) and produced a graph for each. This enables different targets (e.g. 15, 60 and 180 days) to achieve, say, 95% resolution to be set.

The chart shown in figure 7.2 plots the data for problems received this calendar year against the results obtained in the same period of the previous year. This enables the manager to also check whether the situation on the product is changing.

The number of problem reports currently outstanding (see figure 7.3) will vary according to the time since the last release of the product. By monitoring the numbers outstanding, a manager can better judge at what time the next release should be: an earlier release than normal might be justified if a large number of problems are outstanding. Also, the rate of problem reporting can be compared against previous periods to see if the last release was of higher quality. It is unlikely that all problems will be cleared with a new release of the product since some reports will not have had enough time to be processed before the next release.

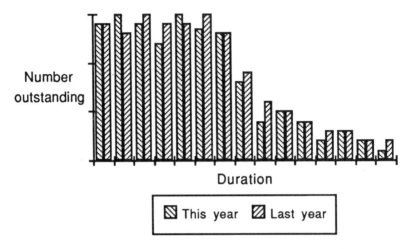

Figure 7.2: Duration that problems have been outstanding

Notes 7.2: The length of time a problem remains outstanding depends on a number of factors, the main ones being cost of implementation and benefit to a customer. It may be worth the manager making further checks on those problems which have been hanging around the longest in order to be sure that customers agree that they are of low priority.

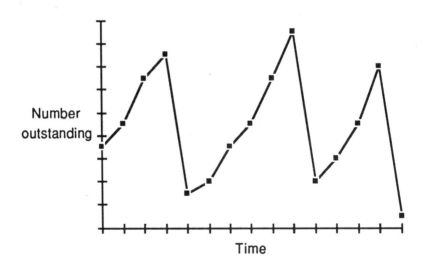

Figure 7.3: Number of problem reports outstanding

THE CUSTOMER'S VIEW OF PRODUCT QUALITY

Simply counting the number of problems outstanding gives a reasonable visibility of customer dissatisfaction. However, these metrics do not take into account the fact that some problems may halt the system, whilst others are only minor irritants to the customer. Thus, to obtain a more accurate measure of the product quality as seen by the customer, a weighting scheme can be applied to the metrics presented above. I have not used one in practice, but a starting point for those interested could be the following:

(1)   System crashes with disastrous consequences   100

(2)   System crashes but can be restarted   30

(3)   Problems for which no user work around is known   10

(4)   Problems which the user can work around   3

(5)   Irritants which the user can get used to   1

I am sure each reader can think of a range of additional factors and weighting values that could be applied to gain a "more accurate" picture of their local situation. In practice, there is no ideal set of weighting factors and they should be set according to the product and customer needs.

CATEGORIES OF PROBLEMS

It seems to be a natural law that most maintenance teams work in permanent overload. This makes it very difficult for the product manager to take effective and proactive actions. The main action is usually to try and recruit, but if a manager takes the time to analyse the staff's activities,ways to improve the team's operations can be highlighted.

For example, the problems reported by customers can be categorised into different types in order to gain better understanding of the major issues that face them. This information can be summarised in a pie chart (see figure 7.4) or monitored over a period using a histogram (see figure 7.5).

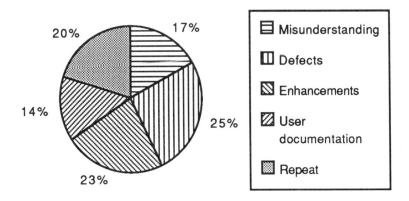

Figure 7.4: Categories of problems reported

Notes 7.4: A misunderstanding means that the customer expected the product to perform differently to its design. No action may be necessary, but a high level of misunderstanding may suggest that user documentation should be enhanced to assist the users in making better use of the product, and reduce the wasted time of the maintenance staff. If the level of repeat reporting of problems is high, the manager should improve feedback to customers on outstanding/known problems.

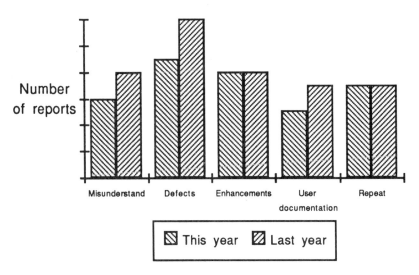

Figure 7.5: Variation of problems reported over time

Notes 7.5: Over the years that a product is in use the type of problems reported will no doubt change. This graph can be used to monitor that change and confirm that maintenance is being effective.

This will provide insight into whether the maintenance team have the right mix of skills and/or whether a change in priorities in the allocation of staff time might lead to a more efficient and effective operation.

Another way in which the problems experienced by customers can be monitored is by categorising the cause of the failure. This is shown in figure 7.6. This analysis might show where the majority of problems lie, enabling preventive maintenance (not a term usually applied to software engineering!) to be performed.

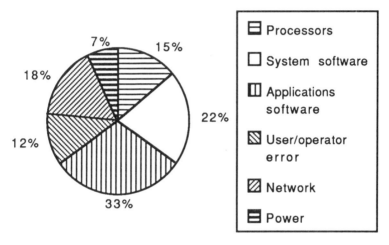

Figure 7.6: Percentage of failures by system component

Notes 7.6: Although software reliability is a difficult concept to measure, this graph can indicate the reliability of the software by comparing it to the hardware reliability.

COST OF MAINTENANCE

It is very important for any manager to monitor the costs of maintenance. This can be done using a variety of graphs. The graph shown in figure 7.7 shows the cost of the changes that have been authorised. If there are many changes at small cost then coordination and scheduling of the changes might be a major management problem; if there are many large changes then the manager is working in an environment which is closer to a normal development. In the latter case, all the metrics described in the previous chapters of this book become more relevant to the maintenance team.

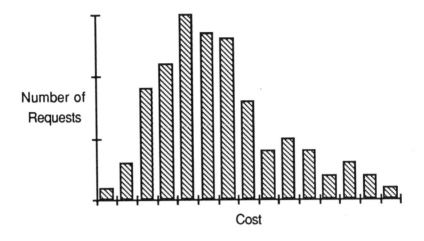

Figure 7.7: Cost of changes

Have you, like me, ever asked what the maintenance team spend all their time doing? The graph in figure 7.8 shows one method for breaking down and making visible the costs of the maintenance team. It can be produced by categorising the types of work they are doing and asking them to complete timesheets. In the example shown, the dominant costs are in evaluating the problem reports and determining what, if any, fault exists. In this example, manpower costs might be able to be reduced by providing additional debugging tools, or implementing some enhancements to the software that will provide improved diagnostics to the evaluators. The cost of the evaluation work will indicate the level of investment in diagnostics that could be cost effective.

By monitoring the current level of rework outstanding the maintenance manager will gain visibility of how well the maintenance team is coping with the backlog of work. The rework outstanding can be split into those activities that must be completed for the next release and those being planned for later releases (work on later releases could be proceeding in parallel to the current release) (see figure 7.9).

Data presented in the format shown in figure 7.9 can also show the rate at which the team is completing work for inclusion in the next release. The trend line can be extrapolated to predict the release date or, more normally, the manager will use this prediction to determine if more, or less changes can be included in the next release.

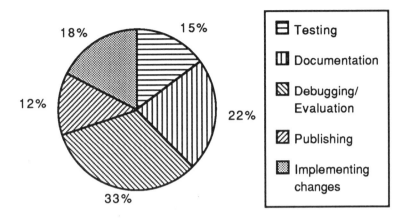

Figure 7.8: Categories of rework

Notes 7.8: This graph was drawn based on the accumulated costs of maintenance over a year. During a period, the type of maintenance will vary and often one change can have a major effect on all costs. It may therefore be appropriate to monitor the costs of rework in categories over many periods and record the data in a histogram. Other categories in which rework may need to be monitored include: software enhancements, performance enhancements, user documentation.

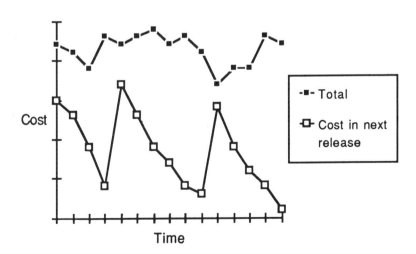

Figure 7.9: Rework outstanding

It might be assumed that the cost of maintenance should reduce after a few years because the product "will have fewer defects" and "the maintenance team will be more efficient." In practice the quality of the product and the effectiveness of maintainers does improve, but there are other factors which can force costs up. One is that the maintenance effort can introduce new faults and another is the type of changes become more complex. One mechanism for monitoring the change in the type of rework occurring is shown in figure 7.10.

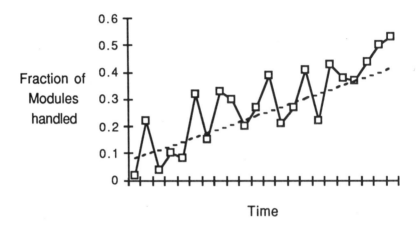

Figure 7.10: Modules handled per release

Notes 7.10: Another way of monitoring the work put into each release could be to monitor the number of lines of code changed in each release. The dotted line shows the trend of the number of modules handled per release.

This graph shows the fraction of modules which have been changed in each release of a software product. The trend line enables a manager to predict the complexity of the next release and to plan for additional staff and tools.

8

Implementing Visibility

MANAGING VISIBILITY

I have been often asked by project managers how to plan and manage visibility on their projects. My answer is summarised in the following list of actions:

(1) Select the metrics that will give you visibility of the key activities on your project.

(2) Prepare the operational procedures, forms, staff organisation and tools for collecting, processing and presenting the metrics you have chosen.

(3) Prepare the staff by educating them on the benefits and practices of metrics collection and visibility and give them some training in the chosen procedures for metrics gathering on your project.

(4) Start collecting and archiving the data. Remember that it may take several months before trends start to provide feedback from some of the graphs.

(5) Arrange for a uniform style of presentation of the results. Include

the team, your manager and the customer in the distribution of
the results.

(6) Use the results, not only to help guide your management of the
project, but also as a sales tool to show your customers how well
you are doing.

These actions are described in detail below and a review of the costs
and benefits of visibility is made.

SELECTING METRICS

The costs of obtaining visibility depend on how much visibility a
project manager wants, i.e. how many metrics are to be collected and
what level of detail is required. Many graphs have been presented in
this book as *examples* of what a project manager could monitor on a
project. There are no doubt many more that have not been covered. A
manager must not assume that all these graphs are needed all of the
time. Nor must it be assumed that any graphs that are used have to
be produced every week. The number of graphs, the detail shown and
the frequency of update will all affect both the level and the costs of
visibility.

What level of visibility should a manager have? Only you can
answer this question as it depends on many characteristics of the
project and its environment, the customer, how long the project has been
running, the problems being faced, and many other factors. The level
of visibility must be decided on a cost benefit basis. Since the benefits
can be hard to quantify (what would it have cost if you had not seen a
problem approaching?), many project managers start off by introducing
a few procedures to gain visibility and, as they gain a better
understanding of how to use them effectively, others are introduced as
needed.

How many metrics should be monitored at any one time on a
project? Well, many of the metrics are only appropriate for certain
phases of the lifecycle and others would only be used if a particular
type of problem needed to be investigated. For example, monitoring
the production of lines of code would only occur during the coding phase
of the project. As an aid to managers who are choosing which metrics
to monitor, a summary of the metrics referred to in this book is given in
table 8.1.

Table 8.1 Summary of techniques

Planning

PERT	Gantt
Activity/resource schedules	Organisation charts
Targets for monitoring progress/quality	

Progress Monitoring

Activities	*Product*
Costs/achievement in each period	Production in each period
(by categories)	(by categories)
Costs accumulated over time	Production accumulated over time
(by categories)	(by categories)
Summary of predictions over time	
Slip chart	

Product Quality

Reviews and change control
Reviews/problems/changes/rework performed in each period (by categories)
Reviews/problems/changes /rework accumulated over time (by categories)
Reviews/problems/changes/rework outstanding in each period (by categories)

Error frequencies	Reviews to success
Faults per module	Effectiveness of clearing problems
Thoroughness of testing	*Other*
Coverage achieved	Call graph
Failures/day	Frequency of use
	Size of modules
	Resource utilisation

Support

Computer facilities utilisation in each period (by categories)
Staff available in each period (by categories)
Staff utilisation in each period (by categories)
Staff turnover in each period (by categories)

Process

Defect fix times	Error rate v. size of module
Cost to repair	Defect density
Changes v phase of detection	Changes v source of defect

Maintenance

Time to respond to problems	Categories of problems and rework
Modules handled per release	

Length of time that problems have been outstanding/numbers outstanding

---

There are many metrics that can be monitored in each phase of a project, but every metric has a cost associated with its data collection. So, as a guideline, I would recommend a manager should consider monitoring only about six metrics initially (see "Introducing Visibility" below). This will enable a range of activities, including progress and quality monitoring, to be covered and any problems on the project should be difficult to miss. If only one or two metrics are monitored then the team might mistakenly assume that all the unmonitored activities are of low priority and can be skipped over quickly. It might also lead the project team into trying to make these metrics look good by, for example, hiding true costs on other activities.

The metrics to be used should be agreed with senior company management and the customer. Project managers are always wary of providing too much information to these people in case their project looks bad because, after all, they can always catch up later, can't they? Those days are gone. The project manager must involve these people in the project because they are the ones who can support the project by providing more resources and/or changing deadlines.

PREPARING THE PROCEDURES

This is the most difficult hurdle for some managers because it means investment of time, but in practice it is not hard to do this. On large projects this task can be delegated as someone's full time responsibility and, for small projects, it is possible to share a common resource, rather than have many people tackle this issue as a part time activity (see "Organisation" below).

In order for the collection and use of metrics to run smoothly, it is recommended that procedures be prepared which answer the following questions:

(1) How is the data to be collected (e.g. timesheets to capture the effort spent on activities, change control forms to capture the nature, cost and impact of a change) and what level of detail is required (e.g to the nearest hour)?

(2) Who is responsible for recording, collecting and analysing the data?

(3) When is the data recorded (e.g. weekly)?

(4) How is the data to be analysed and presented (e.g. using graphs), and when does this happen (e.g. monthly)?

You will often find that the times when visibility gives you most benefit (e.g. demanding requirements with tight deadlines) are precisely those in which there is little effort to be spared for data collection. Hence, simple data collection procedures, automated data capture and no duplication of data entry are important features of a data collection system. Also, maintaining the integrity of a large database of project metrics can become a full time job in itself unless adequate safeguards are employed.

I have said little about statistical analysis techniques in this book because these are techniques which project managers will normally call upon rather than have within their own skills. Knowledge of statistical analysis techniques will be required for the more complex metrics (e.g. to measure the degree to which exceptional points diverge from the norm), but (to be honest) I have never found the need to use them on my projects.

Automation

There are more and more tools appearing on the market to help managers in their job. Some examples of the types of tools that can help provide visibility are:

- tools to aid estimation of project costs;

- tools to aid planning and scheduling;

- tools to accumulate and analyse costs;

- tools to produce graphs and statistical analysis.

I am not going to review all the products available, but it is worth noting a few characteristics to look for when buying tools. To a large extent, you get what you pay for. For example, a small project (say, less than 10 people) can monitor costs and analyse them using a simple spreadsheet costing less than a thousand dollars. On the other hand, large financial packages are required to monitor large projects and provide the detailed analysis required for company auditing purposes. These could set you back over $100,000.

In order to obtain effective project control, the actual costs need to be compared against the plans and the original estimates. If the manager has bought a cost estimating tool, a planning tool and a cost monitoring tool then data will have to be transferred between tools or even the output from one tool retyped as input data for another. A much better approach is to buy one tool which provides all these functions without the need to duplicate any data.

More comprehensive automation can be obtained if an Integrated Project Support Environment (IPSE) is used during the development and maintenance work. This would allow the operation of all development tools to automatically update a central database with information about their use. For example, each use of the compiler could be recorded, or configuration management information about the production of products could be compared against plans. Such a toolset will be of great use to a manager who wants visibility of his project, but this technology is still in its early days of use.

All this talk about automation may persuade some people that it is necessary to use tools to obtain visibility. Far from it. Consider, for example, change control procedures. These require forms (paper or computer based) to be filled in when changes to authorised components are required. In this example, simple counts of the outstanding forms and the addition of only one point on a graph each week or month is all that is required to maintain the graph shown in figure 4.15. This can easily be done by hand without any automated support at all and it is typical of the effort required to maintain many of the graphs.

Organisation

The organisational structure on a project can affect the visibility a manager needs. In practice, managers often set up an organisation structure at the start of a project and leave it unchanged until the completion of work. However, as the project progresses, the work changes and the requirements for visibility and control change with it.

An example may help the understanding of this point. A typical project organisation structure used to help coordination of design effort is shown in figure 8.1. If this structure is used in the test and integration phase of the project then each team will be responsible for testing and correcting faults in the software it developed. This can be a very effective way of working since it has the advantage that the designer of some software should be able to trace faults and correct them much faster than anyone else.

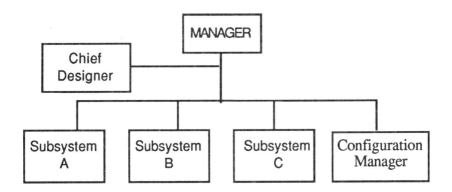

Figure 8.1: Organisation chart in the design phase of a project

However, this structure does make it very difficult for the manager to monitor the team's activities because:

(1) Staff are moving quickly between design, test, debug and error correction activities. It will be difficult for them to produce accurate statistics for the time spent on each activity.

(2) Staff will be loath to fill out "lots of paperwork" reporting each fault and obtaining approval for its correction. With good intentions, staff will try to save the project's time and resources by correcting faults on their own initiative "without all the paperwork".

Although the staff often prefer this way of working, and it does appear to be efficient, it can lead the project in to serious difficulty. Without visibility, the project manager does not have control. If the project manager could obtain accurate visibility of the work of the staff in this phase then:

(1) Knowing the proportions of time spent testing, debugging, reworking software, a bottleneck in the process that the manager could clear may be highlighted.

(2) Knowing the number and types of faults and their rate of detection will assist the manager in predicting the release date for the software and it may highlight weaknesses in the development process.

One mechanism the manager can use to improve visibility in the test and integration phase is to reorganise the team so that the development and rework effort is separated from the test and integration effort (see figure 8.2). The function of the configuration manager is to authorise all rework performed by the development team and to monitor all new products in order to ensure the test and integration team have a consistent set of components.

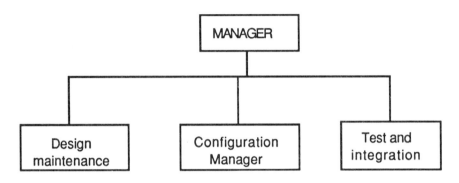

Figure 8.2: Organisation chart in the test and integration phase of a project

Whereas the information flow shown in figure 8.2 may be that desired by the project manager when the team was organised according to the structure shown in figure 8.1, it is only by the clear separation of work and responsibilities that the desired visibility and control will be achieved. The staff will be only too quick to point out the "inefficiency" in the new structure, so the project manager must be prepared to defend the advantages gained by the visibility provided.

The metrics collected on a project mainly originate from the work of the team members and are accumulated for action by the project manager. Team members might be wary of this procedure if they distrust how the manager might use the information. This problem can be reduced by setting up a metrics team (this could be a part time role in small organisations). The project team members are usually happy to present metrics to a metrics team since they are only helping the metrics team do their job. The metrics team will process the data and present graphs and statistics to the managers and team members. Another advantage of using a metrics team is that they will accumulate information from several projects and help disseminate this knowledge more widely.

PREPARING PEOPLE

The metrics collected on a project depend on the project team for providing accurate and timely information. If the team do not recognise the benefits of collecting metrics, the metrics collected are likely to be wholly inaccurate. In order to have the support of the team, the manager must involve them in the metrics planning and analysis.

Team members are often very suspicious of metrics because it is felt that they may be used as "a rod to beat them". In order to overcome this, managers should avoid using metrics to monitor and criticise individuals. It is interesting to note that when metrics are used to monitor a team's efforts, the team are motivated to work together to obtain good results. This motivation can be increased by posting the metrics on the office walls. Although some managers would rather avoid this because "the customer might see them", the motivation and involvement of the team is crucial to the success of metrics.

Many elements of visibility will be based on reports provided by the staff. Unless the manager can persuade them to be scrupulously honest, the visibility will be corrupted. I'm not saying that some staff will tell lies, just that some staff don't like to tell a manager what he doesn't want to hear. They think that, by delaying the truth, they will be able to overcome the problem themselves without anyone else needing to know. Such action might be done for good reasons, but it restricts the visibility of the manager and hence his ability to do his job effectively. Hence, the catch phrase of the project should be "honesty is the best policy". The team should be encouraged to participate in setting measurable targets, thus avoiding woolly thinking and ambiguous goals.

During the project the project team should be encouraged to be as honest as possible with their recording of time. Monitoring every few minutes of activity is not essential for overall accuracy, but if a person works more or less hours in the standard week then it should be recorded. Too often tasks are forgotten from the plans and overconscientious staff perform them in unbooked overtime. If this happens then the metrics will be incorrect and subsequent projects are likely to face the same problems again. Also, when tasks are being monitored, they should not be recorded as complete until the task is properly completed. Too often projects find themselves in the "90% complete" syndrome because in the final weeks of the project staff tidy up all those little pieces of work that were not completed earlier.

Another problem is that keen staff are often prepared to put in a few extra hours to resolve a problem, without reporting the cost to the "system". Whilst this might be praiseworthy, it will result in inaccurate information being supplied to the manager and might lead to further inaccurate estimates in the future.

To overcome the initial reluctance of a team to use metrics, and to ensure that they help to ensure the accuracy of the results, the manager should organise a short seminar for the staff. The objective of this seminar is to educate the team as to the benefits of metrics, to teach them some of the principles of data collection (e.g. how to choose between categories for certain data) and to gain their support in making the process of metrics collection effective. In my experience, bringing together the team for a seminar like this can require a whole day to ensure the effective introduction of visibility to a project.

INTRODUCING VISIBILITY

Most of the metrics presented in this book are easy to collect, so why are more people not collecting them? One major factor is that it does take some management time immediately; it's the old "costs now for benefits later" problem. Even when managers recognise the benefits to be obtained by using metrics, there is the worry about what the real cost of obtaining metrics is. I would recommend in this situation that a couple of pilot projects be started to demonstrate the benefits of metrics in use. These should be allowed to run for up to 6 months so that other projects can see the costs and benefits in practice. I have suggested 6 months is needed because over the first 3 months the costs are visible, but the benefits are not since there is insufficient data to overcome the noise in the metrics and to detect trends. After 6 months there is enough data to detect real trends and by this time the project team is usually so involved with metrics that they are eagerly awaiting the next set of figures.

How should the metrics be reported? In order to involve the team, one copy of the graphs should be posted on the office walls for all to see. However, for management purposes it is possible and appropriate to photo-reduce up to 6 graphs onto one piece of A4 paper. (See example shown in figure 8.3. These graphs are not all from the same project at the same instant in time.) You may think that this makes them impossible to read, but a manager will soon find that a graph is not used to show details. It is the profiles that matter.

When a manager uses graphs to provide visibility then, instead of reading long project reports which go into some detail about what happened last month, the profile of the graph will quickly indicate if anything is going wrong and the size of any action required. If the profiles are reasonable then a quick glance is the only management time needed. If there is a problem, then a written report in support of the graphs should concentrate on *what action is required and the impact on forward plans*. My experience with this approach is that the use of graphs dramatically alters and improves the style of management reporting. People concentrate on what action needs to be taken to improve the future outlook, rather than dwelling on what has happened in the past.

Which graphs should a project start using first? Well, to some extent, this will depend on the phase the project is currently in, but those graphs shown in figure 8.3 are some that I use most often. The reason I have chosen this set is:

(1) The Gantt chart shows details of activities and what activities should be happening this week on the project. The slip line gives a very visual representation of the slippage on the project and which activities are falling behind schedule.

(2) The chart showing planned, actual and earned progress is a concise summary of the costs on the project and is a powerful indicator of trends and forecast end date.

(3) The weekly costs chart shows the type of work the team are doing, the proportion of spend in each type of activity and provides an overall guide as to the weekly costs of the project.

(4) The graph showing a correlation of the estimated costs of activities against the actual costs gives very useful feedback to the planners on the accuracy of their planning. It is also quite motivating to the project team who do try to make this graph look good.

(5) The graph showing cumulative problems and changes indicates how well the quality control procedures are operating. For example, if the rate of reporting problems flattens off, I check that the team are not cutting corners by not performing reviews or tests.

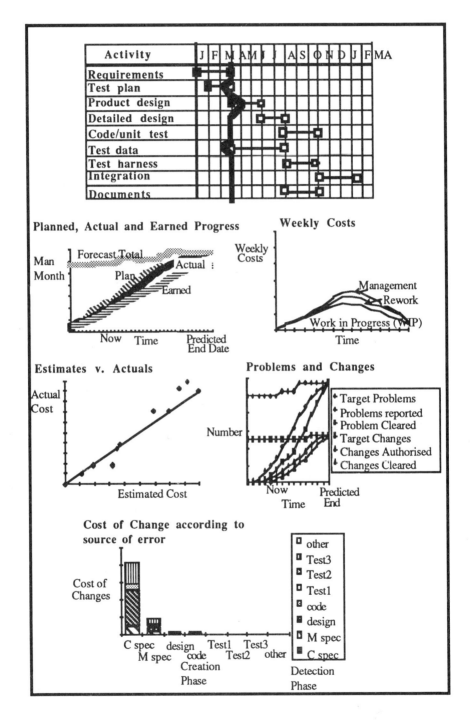

Figure 8.3: Example of a graphical progress report

(6) The histogram showing cost of change is not too useful until the end of the project, but I have included it here because it can be very important to a project manager to have visibility of the causes of the project's rework activities.

One other graph which I would strongly recommend if the project is in the testing phase is the one which monitors the number of test cases produced, executed and completed. It has been very helpful to me on several projects to help manage and plan testing.

REPLANNING

As the project progresses, activities will be completed early or late, and the manager will have a better understanding of the work to be done in the future. Each change to the estimates, or completion of an activity permits the project manager to reschedule the activities on the project to see what, if any, the repercussions are. This process can be a valuable aid to the manager, but it can also mean that he spends more time rescheduling than managing!

Each time the project is rescheduled, the manager should advise the development team by issuing a new copy of the plans. However, if this is done too frequently it will demotivate the team who like to work to a fixed target. However, delays in issuing an updated plan will mean that many aspects of the current plan are out of date and might lead to confusion in the team. Experience will determine the best time for a manager to issue new plans, but typically this will be between 3 and 6 months after the previous release.

END OF PROJECT REVIEWS

Many of the benefits of implementing visibility will be lost if the information is not collected at the end of a project. All of the initial estimates, together with the initial assumptions and actual results, should be compiled together and reviewed by the project team and management. Many of the graphs shown in Chapter 6 can be used to assist the analysis.

A review meeting can investigate the metrics and any conclusions on how the project could have been improved should be circulated to other project managers so that the knowledge is not lost. Do not forget to set the project in context when analysing the results. Consider, inter alia, project requirements, scope, complexity and special features. Also, do not forget to review projects that have failed. Reviews of failed projects are often the most useful in setting guidelines for other projects.

When should an end of project review occur? One review should occur after first delivery has taken place, but that is not the end of the project because work will continue on maintenance and enhancement. I recommend that reviews are held annually after the first delivery to review the impact of maintenance and new releases on the product.

COSTS

There is no fixed cost associated with obtaining visibility, but to a large extent, a manager will only get what is paid for. If a manager decides that his control will be improved by receiving lots of graphs to a fine level of detail then this can be achieved. It will require plans to be prepared at the detail required and the development activities to be monitored closely to obtain the data. This must then be gathered together, analysed and distributed to the interested parties.

My experience suggests the typical costs of obtaining visibility is from 3 to 6% of total project costs. This is in addition to the costs of estimating and planning which themselves may also be 2 to 4% of total costs. On a small project these costs might be born by several individuals, whereas on a large project a small team can be assigned the task full time. Much of these costs are not new. Many projects already monitor their work through the use of timesheets and change control forms. However, few organisations provide the analysis of the material they collect or even accumulate it so that it can be analysed at the end of a project. Improving the visibility that a project manager has is a small cost compared to the risk of poor control and project overrun.

On a large project where the tasks have been assigned to full time individuals, the costs of obtaining visibility are themselves very visible. Not only that, but these tasks are often boring chores, not directly producing for the project. I once worked on a project which was running close to budget so the manager decided that these visible, apparently non-productive costs could be cut to save money. He forgot that this also cut his visibility of the project, leaving him "blind" and with no control of the project. You may not be surprised to learn that 2 weeks before planned delivery, the project manager informed the customer that a recent review of the project showed six months of work still remained. Since this was an 80 person project, 40 man-years had been "lost" because the manager had no visibility.

BENEFITS

The use of visibility on a project must be planned and controlled if its benefits are to be realised. This means that data collection activities must be managed and that tools and procedures for data collection, storage and analysis must be provided. The benefits of visibility accrue throughout the lifecycle of development and maintenance. At the start of a project developers will be able to provide more accurate and justifiable estimates and avoid taking on projects which have little chance of success. During the project the manager will

(1) have good plans of the resources required in order to achieve deadlines and budgets;

(2) make timely, effective decisions when progress deviates from the plans;

(3) identify potential problems early and take preemptive action to minimise their impact.

Customers will see the benefits of metrics in the improved accuracy of cost and schedule estimates with an improving quality level.

In my experience, the introduction of metrics has had far reaching consequences. The improved visibility changes the attitudes of the whole project team, because they receive feedback on what they have been doing and on their progress towards a goal. This results in a more even work pattern during the project, rather then the easy going attitude that can occur early in a project, followed by the working of excessive hours as the delivery date looms.

The use of metrics also facilitates senior management who use the metrics to identify anomalies between projects and to see the impact of new tools and techniques in the organisation. For example, if one project is spending more time on integration testing then their design techniques may have flaws. As a result of the availability of metrics, management are often spurred into making changes to make their company more competitive. I have tried to promote change top-down in the past and found it very hard work. However, after introducing metrics to a project, I found that a bottom-up push to change working practices followed because the metrics showed the staff that there was a need for change.

WHAT NEXT?

Hopefully this book has stimulated many ideas in the mind of the reader, but turning these into project practices can be quite a challenge. To summarise, some of the actions you must consider in order to introduce metrics successfully are:

- Decide which metrics/graphs you wish to use initially, together with the accuracy and frequency of data collection. No more than 6 metrics are recommended to start with.

- Prepare Work Breakdown Structure, plans and set targets. See Chapter 2 for some guidelines, but a lot will depend on local practice, tools and the metrics you have chosen.

- Set up data collection procedures to support the metrics you have chosen. These can be timesheets to collect data about costs, forms for change control, etc.

- Educate the project team to understand the benefits to be gained by monitoring metrics to ensure you have their support in providing accurate data.

- Collect the data, analyse it and make the results known to the team.

Don't forget that some care should be taken when using the results. For example, the metrics may indicate there are no problems even when some exist: be aware of their limitations. Alternatively, some metrics may indicate there is a problem when there may be a simple cause, e.g. Christmas holidays always cause a hiccup in the profiles.

The relationship between the primary activities is shown in figure 8.4.

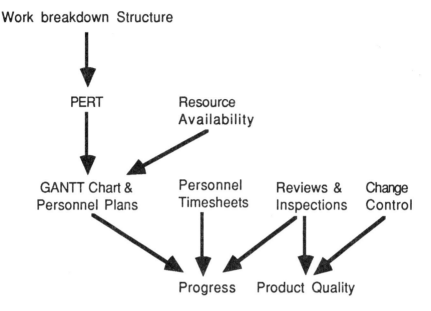

Figure 8.4: Primary activities to obtain visibility

This book only tackles a small part of the role of project managers. Some books which expand on some of the issues which are just touched upon here are:

Barry W Boehm (1981) *Software Engineering Economics* Prentice-Hall

R Grady and D Caswell (1987) *Software Metrics. Establishing a Company Wide Program* Prentice-Hall

Jeffrey Keen (1987) *Managing Systems Development* Wiley

Tom de Marco (1987) *Controlling Software Projects* Yourdon Press

Tom Gilb (1988) *Principles of Software Engineering Management* Addison Wesley

There are also many articles in the literature on the topic of using metrics to monitor software development. For those of you who wish to investigate this topic further, a good starting point would be the

March, 1990 issue of the IEEE magazine *Software* which takes the subject of metrics as its main theme. It includes several review articles with references to key articles in the literature.

CONCLUSIONS

This book has presented an approach which will help project managers gain visibility of what is happening on their projects. Examples have been presented of specific mechanisms by which visibility can be obtained, but the reader is encouraged to use these as suggestions and guidelines, rather than treating them as the only solutions available.

Visibility is only as good as the data provided. Many of the techniques to obtain visibility give direct, unambiguous, factual results, so long as certain checks are performed. In order for visibility to be successful, the project staff must be persuaded that "honesty is the best policy" (i.e. they must believe in the benefits of visibility), reporting mechanisms should encourage honesty within the project and checks should be made by the quality assurance team.

Achieving accurate visibility can not be achieved without some small and very visible cost. The manager must be prepared to accept these costs in return for the improved control that visibility provides.

APPENDIX

CHOOSING AND USING GRAPHS

There is a wide variety of graphical representations of data that can aid a project manager. The data collected from a project contains many messages, but our objective is to find the most significant messages and to display them clearly. In this Appendix we will review the forms available for displaying information and consider when they may be used. When a project manager comes to choose a format, answers to the following questions will help the choice:

- What is the most critical information to be displayed?

- How is the data changing?

- What predictions can be made?

- How significant are the trends?

On a project, many of the types of data collected are varying over time, but there are other comparisons that can be made, e.g.

(1) comparison of components to the whole;

(2) comparison of components;

(3)   comparison of one or more items over time;

(4)   Co-relationship between variations.

Before selecting the type of graph to use, a manager must decide what visibility is required and how it can be best presented.

There are four basic forms of a graph: pie, bar (or column), curve and scatter. The choice of which one to use depends both on the comparison to be made and the type of data to be analysed. The matrix shown below (see Table A.1) indicates the most appropriate forms for each type of comparison.

Table A.1: Choosing a graph format for a comparison

	Pie	Bar	Curve	Scatter
Components to whole	*	*		
Components		*		
Time		*	*	
Co-relation		*		*

A number of variations from the basic formats are available to emphasise particular types of comparison. For example, several curves can be shown on the same graph. Also, several forms can be combined onto one display e.g. a column graph which shows period by period quantities can be combined with a curve that shows cumulative totals. Of course, combining graphs soon leads to a situation in which the reader can be confused by too much information. The basic recommendation is: keep your charts simple until you and your team have the experience to use more complex analysis.

COMPARISON OF COMPONENTS TO THE WHOLE

This type of graph is used to compare the contribution (share, percentage) of components to the whole. The most common mechanism for this is the pie chart because a circle gives a clear impression of the whole and the "slices of the pie" show the relative sizes of the components (see figure A.1).

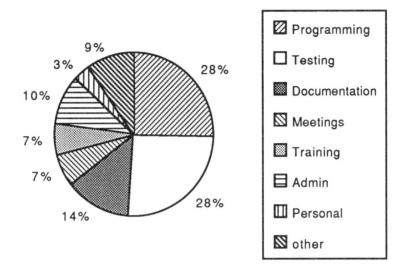

Figure A.1: A pie chart

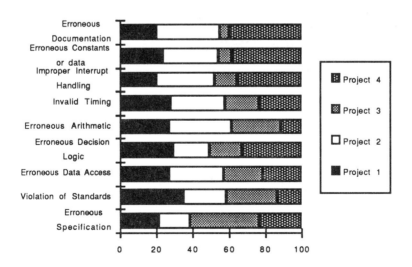

Figure A.2: 100% bar chart

A pie chart is most expressive when there are only a few components. Because the eye is used to measuring in clockwise motion, the most important segment should normally be positioned against the 12 o'clock line. Components can be emphasised by shading or by withdrawing a segment from the pie.

It is frequently necessary to compare the component sizes across several totals. For this, a bar chart with each bar at 100% is better suited because the bars can be easily compared and labelled (see figure A.2).

A bar chart can be drawn with the bars either vertical (columns) or horizontal. A horizontal bar chart is usually best because there is more space for labelling and an audience might incorrectly assume that there is a time sequence when the bars are vertical.

COMPARISON OF ITEMS

This comparison is used when there are several items to be compared against each other, rather than a total. For this type of comparison a bar chart is appropriate (see figure A.3). Sequencing the bars from high to low values can be an aid to the reader to emphasise a relationship between categories of data.

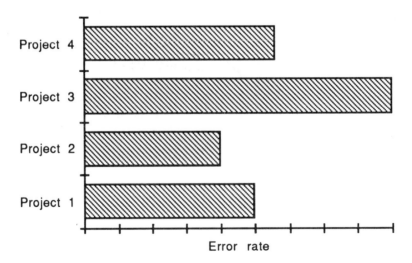

Figure A.3: Bar chart

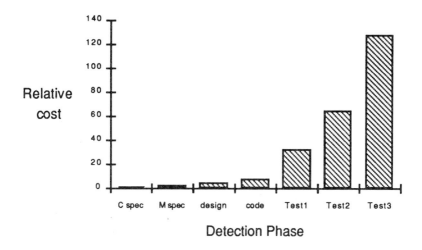

Figure A.4: Column chart

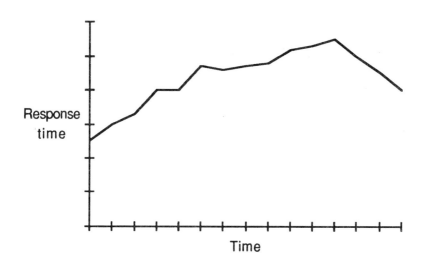

Figure A.5: Curve graph

COMPARISON OF ITEMS OVER TIME

This sort of graph is used to highlight trends, fluctuations and patterns of change over time. For these types of comparison, it is better to use a column chart when there are a few time periods to be plotted, when there is extreme variability in the data to be plotted, or when the data has been measured in (possibly overlapping) time intervals (see figure A.4). A curve graph is better when many points are to be plotted and/or when the data points reflect a continuity in time (see figure A.5).

When several curves are to be shown on the same graph it can be appropriate to add each new series of data to the previous values and shade the intervening area (see figure A.6). This technique can make it difficult to compare the relative sizes of points in each series, but it does show how the data accumulates.

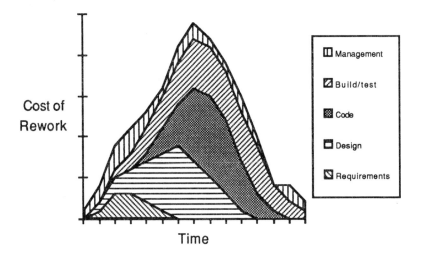

Figure A.6: Shaded curve graph

CO-RELATIONSHIP BETWEEN VARIATIONS

This type of comparison shows how variation in one respect relates to variation in another for the purpose of determining whether the relationship follows a meaningful pattern. A scatter diagram (see figure A.7) is suited to this purpose when there are many points to be compared. It is often useful to include a curve on the graph to point out what the expected pattern should be, or to show a "line of best fit".

When there are only a few data values to be compared and there is no sequence to the data, a paired bar chart can be used. One of the coordinates, usually the independent variable, identifies the bars and the dependent variable is used to specify the length of the bar.

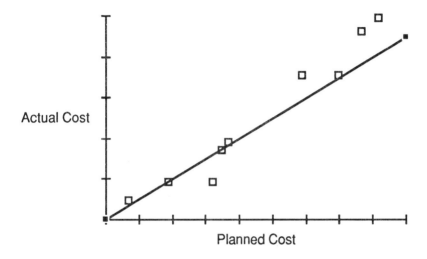

Figure A.7: Scatter diagram

SUMMARY

The comparison(s) are chosen by you. There are several graphical techniques which you can use to make the best use of the data available. Just as with your choice of data, the choice of the graph to present the data can mislead the interpretation. Omitting key facts, overemphasising data by manipulation of the scales on a graph, or making predictions on trends which have little statistical significance can lead you or your management into erroneous action. *Use these tools with care.*

INDEX

Acceptance, 98
Accommodation, 103
Achievement, 49
Activities, 20
Administration, 106
Automation, 137
Availability, 5, 97

Balls on the walls, 46-47
Bar chart, 153
Boehm, B.W., 149
Budgets, 23, 55

Call graph, 95
Caswell, D., 149
Categories
    of changes, 87
    of costs, 50
    of defect, 72
    of problems, 87, 127-128

of production, 53
    of rework, 88, 131
Change, 77-90
Closed loop control, 8
Code, lines of, 58, 92
Column chart, 155
Communication lines, 101
Competitive advantage, 6
Compilation, 58
Complexity, 59, 91
Component, 58
Configuration management, 109
Contingency, 24, 39, 54
Cost
    accumulated over time, 53
    of change, 115, 128
    in a period
Cost-benefit, 40
Creation phase, 119
Critical path, 5, 27
Curve graph, 155
Customer specification, 115

Deadlines, 23
Debug, 61
Defect, 63, 70-72, 78, 93, 109, 111
       density, 114
       fix times, 121
Delivery date, 4
Design, 60, 112
Design maintenance, 140
Detection phase, 115
Disk space, 101
Document, 58, 101

Earned value, 52-53
Effectiveness of clearing problems,
   89
End date, 55,63
Engineering, 107
Enhancements, 128
Estimates, 17, 21, 22, 44, 48
Events, 22

Facilities, 101
Failures over time, 76
Forms
            for change control, 80
            for problem reports, 79

Gantt, 32
Gilb, T., 149
Grady, R., 149

Halstead, 90
Hardware, 57, 87
Holidays

Implementation, 112, 133-150

Integration, 112
Interfaces, 72

Keen, J., 149

Lifecycle, 111

Maintenance, 5, 7, 117-132, 135
Management, 54, 112
Marco, T. W., 149
McCabe, 90
Meetings, 106
Method, 109
Misunderstanding, 128
Model, 24
Module, 58, 89, 132
Mutation, 77

Network, 129

Organisation, 35, 109, 138-140

Paths, 67
People, 141
Performance, 97
Peripherals, 7
Personnel, 33
PERT, 26-8
Phase, 81, 110
Pie chart, 153
Plans/Planning, 6, 17-42, 48, 135
Predictions over time, 56
Problem, 77-90, 117-126
Procedures, 136-140
Process, 6, 7, 109-121, 135

Processor, 102
Product, 7, 23, 127, 135
Production, 59-60
    accumulated over time, 38
    in a period, 58
Profit, 54
Programming, 61, 106
Progress, 6, 43-64, 67, 135, 144
Project, 110, 145

Quality, 20, 36, 63-100, 127, 135
Quality Assurance, 103, 111

Recruitment, 103
Release, 75, 99, 132
Reliability, 4, 6, 97
Replanning, 145
Resources, 21, 45, 49, 51, 97, 101, 106, 120
Response time, 84, 118
Reuse, 94
Review, 23, 59, 67-77
Rework, 23, 39,49, 54, 59, 82, 83, 88, 113, 131
Risk, 24

Scatter diagram, 157
Schedule, 20, 29-31
Shaded curve graph, 156
Size, 92
Skills, 105
Slip charts, 45
Specification, 112
Staff

available, 105
    joining and leaving
    profiles, 27
    turnover, 105
    utilisation, 106
Statistical control, 113
Structure, 58, 95-96
Structure diagram, 96
Sub-contracts, 101, 107
Supplies, 103
Support, 5, 101-107, 135
System, 97, 121, 128

Targets, 25
Tasks *see Activities*
Test data, 58, 62
Test specification, 58
Testing, thoroughness, coverage, 63, 67-77, 140
Timesheets, 146
Tools, 109
Training, 103

Unit tests, 61
User documentation, 128

Verification and validation, 4

Work Breakdown Structure, 26-27
Work in progress, 49